THE PUZZLE OF MODERN ECONOMICS

Is economics the key to everything or does the recent financial crisis show that it has failed? This book provides an assessment of modern economics that cuts through the confusion and controversy over this question. Case studies of the creation of new markets, the Russian transition to capitalism, globalization, and money and finance establish that economics has been very successful where problems have been well defined and where the world can be changed to fit the theory, but that it has been less successful in tackling bigger problems. The book then offers a historical perspective on how, since the Second World War, economists have tried to make their subject scientific. It explores the evolving relationship between science and ideology and investigates the place of heterodoxy and dissent within the discipline. It is argued that, though there are problems with the discipline, economics is needed to combat the myths that abound concerning economic problems.

Roger E. Backhouse is Professor of the History and Philosophy of Economics at the University of Birmingham, where he has taught since 1980, and at Erasmus University Rotterdam. In 2007, he was Ludwig Lachmann Research Fellow in the Department of Philosophy at the London School of Economics. From 1998 to 2000, he held a British Academy Research Readership. He has also taught at University College London, University of Keele, the University of Bristol, the University of Buckingham and the University of Oporto.

Professor Backhouse is the co-editor of *The History of the Social Sciences Since 1945*, with Philippe Fontaine (Cambridge University Press, 2010); *No Wealth But Life: Welfare Economics and the Welfare State in Britain 1880–1945*, with Tamotsu Nishizawa (Cambridge University Press, 2010), and *The Unsocial Social Science? Economics and Neighboring Disciplines Since 1945* (forthcoming). He also co-edited, with Bradley W. Bateman, *The Cambridge Companion to Keynes* (Cambridge University Press, 2006). Professor Backhouse is also author of *The Ordinary Business of Life* and *The Penguin History of Economics*. He has written for a number of journals, including *Economica*, *Journal of Economic Perspectives*, *History of Political Economy*, *Journal of the History of Economic Thought*, and *Journal of Economic Methodology*. He has been review editor of the *Economic Journal*, editor of the *Journal of Economic Methodology*, and associate editor of the *Journal of the History of Economic Thought*.

The Puzzle of Modern Economics

Science or Ideology?

ROGER E. BACKHOUSE

University of Birmingham and
Erasmus University Rotterdam

CAMBRIDGE
UNIVERSITY PRESS

CAMBRIDGE UNIVERSITY PRESS
Cambridge, New York, Melbourne, Madrid, Cape Town, Singapore,
São Paulo, Delhi, Dubai, Tokyo, Mexico City

Cambridge University Press
32 Avenue of the Americas, New York, NY 10013-2473, USA

www.cambridge.org
Information on this title: www.cambridge.org/9780521532617

First published 2010

Printed in the United States of America

A catalog record for this publication is available from the British Library.

Library of Congress Cataloging in Publication data
Backhouse, Roger, 1951–
The puzzle of modern economics : science or ideology / Roger E. Backhouse.
p. cm.
Includes bibliographical references and index.
ISBN 978-0-521-82554-2 (hardback)
1. Economics – History – 20th century.   2. Economic policy – History – 20th century.
I. Title.
HB87.B235 2010
330–dc22   2010014788

ISBN 978-0-521-82554-2 Hardback
ISBN 978-0-521-53261-7 Paperback

Contents

Acknowledgements

Writing this book has taken a long time. The original idea was for a book that used an account of the recent history of economics (since the Second World War) to shed light on the current state of the discipline. My hope was that I could prepare a book fairly quickly by drawing on work that I have been doing on this subject over the past decade. However, though a draft was assembled very quickly, it was unsatisfactory, and work stalled partly because of other projects but mainly because I could not get the various pieces to fit together as I had hoped. Many drafts later, this is the result, with many of the original chapters cut away and replaced with new ones, leaving a book that is as much methodological as historical.

Though my hope is that the book will contribute to debates within the economics profession, and though I can see many ideas in the economic methodology literature lying behind remarks I make, I decided that the main ideas could and therefore should (an unconventional view) be presented in such a way as to be accessible to non-economists or, should that prove overoptimistic, to those who studied 'Economics 101' in the distant past. I therefore ask my economist colleagues to be patient when I explain material that they will find very elementary. At the same time, non-economists will encounter abstract material, and I ask such readers to try to see the picture that lies behind any difficult theoretical ideas.

I have accumulated many debts in the course of the work that led to this book. Amongst those whose work framed my way of thinking about these problems, I would pick out the late Bob Coats, without whose encouragement and persuasion, I might never have started to think about the questions in which this project originated. Mark Blaug and Kevin Hoover have been important in influencing the ideas on empirical work expressed here, and papers written for volumes edited by Uskali Mäki and Marcel Boumans were more important than citations alone might suggest.

The main reason I have been able to progress from the original manuscript to the present one is that I have received strong criticisms from readers. Mark Blaug, Kevin Hoover, Steven Medema, and two readers who remain anonymous read an early draft of the manuscript and provided helpful comments. Bradley Bateman offered invaluable advice on key chapters and willingly discussed many ideas with me. Philip Hanson and Robert Wade also offered useful advice on specific chapters.

However, my major academic debts (the non-academic debt to my wife Ann will be obvious to anyone who has engaged in such a long project) are to Scott Parris, my patient editor at Cambridge University Press, who provided detailed comments on more than one draft, and guided me as I sought to restructure the manuscript, and to Steven Medema. He and I worked out key ideas in papers we wrote together, and we have conducted a long-running discussion on economists and the market, centred on his recent book *The Hesitant Hand* as well as on what we have been doing together. Not only has he commented on the whole draft, but he has read multiple versions of several chapters, trying, though not always succeeding, to keep me on the straight and narrow.

R. E. B.

November 2009

1

Introduction

WHY DID NO ONE SEE IT COMING?

On 5 November 2008, Her Majesty Queen Elizabeth II was opening a new building at the London School of Economics. Speaking of the credit crunch, she turned to some of the economists present and said, 'It's awful. Why did no one see it coming?' Journalists, not constrained to be diplomatic, were more forthright in condemning economists. For Anatol Kaletsky, one-time economics editor of the *Times*, 'Economists are the guilty men' (the *Times* 5 February 2009). The economics editor of the *Guardian*, Larry Elliott, claimed that 'as a profession, economics not only has nothing to say about what caused the world to come to the brink of financial collapse ... but also a supreme lack of interest' (the *Guardian* 1 June 2009). Writing in the same newspaper, Simon Jenkins attributed this failure to the fact that 'Economists regard it as their duty fearlessly to offer government what it wants to hear. ... Don't rock the boat, says the modern profession, and the indexed pension is secure.' The whole economics profession, he contended, had 'suffered a collapse' (12 November 2008).

Even more significantly, prominent economists have argued that the profession has gone astray. Nobel Laureate Paul Krugman, whose academic career has taken him through some of the world's leading economics departments – MIT, Yale and Princeton – has endorsed the view that blame for the crisis falls on economists as well as on financiers, bankers and policy makers. His assessment is that 'the economics profession went astray because economists, as a group, mistook beauty, clad in impressive-looking mathematics, for truth' (*New York Times* 6 September 2009).

The charge is serious because Krugman is arguing not just that economists got something wrong but also that their failure was deeply rooted
in values that are at the heart of the profession.

These are not isolated criticisms. They reflect widely held attitudes,
not just in Britain, but also in the United States, Europe and, no doubt,
in most countries affected by the economic crisis. Following one of the
biggest economic policy failures since the 1930s, the economics profession is getting a bad press. Yet only a few years ago, the image it presented to the public was very different – that of a discipline that was not
just successful but also overflowing with confidence. Economics was the
key to understanding everything, as the titles appearing in bookstalls
revealed: *Everlasting Light Bulbs: How Economics Illuminates the World*
(Kay 2004); *Freakonomics: A Rogue Economist Explains the Hidden
Side of Everything* (Levitt and Dubner 2006); *More Sex Is Safer Sex: The
Unconventional Wisdom of Economics* (Landsburg 2007); *The Logic of
Life: The New Economics of Everything* (Harford 2008); *The Economic
Naturalist: Why Economics Explains Almost Everything* (Frank 2008).

The changed attitude towards economics is hardly surprising. The
forces that drive the economy from boom to depression and back again
remain a mystery to most people. In times of prosperity, people can leave
esoteric matters, such as credit default swaps, collateralized debt obligations or the London inter-bank lending rate, to the professionals, trust-
ing that they know what they are doing. It is only when something goes
wrong that questions are asked and people demand explanations of why
billions of dollars, euros and pounds of taxpayers' money are suddenly
being poured in to prop up the financial system.

Yet there is more to it than this; criticism of economics did not begin
with the banking crisis of July to September 2007. Far from it, there had
long been unease about economics. Thus Diane Coyle, one-time economics editor of the *Independent* and the author of *Sex, Drugs and Economics* (2004), a book in the 'economics is the key to everything' vein,
saw a need to put the record straight. Economics, according to the title of
her second book, was not the 'dismal science' – it was *The Soulful Science*
(2007). Shunning the popular themes of her previous book, she explained
that economists had begun to understand the role of innovation in economic growth and how to design policies that would eventually make

poverty history. Critics of economics, she argued, simply did not understand the subject.

Coyle's target was what she called the 'policy intelligensia', a term covering those who write in opinion columns in the *New York Times*, the *Guardian* or *Le Monde*, or the longer, seemingly more serious, pieces emanating from policy think tanks or published in *New Republic* or the *Nation*. In the aftermath of a financial crisis that precipitated a depression, her claims may look over-optimistic; nevertheless she hits many of her targets. What she missed, however, is the fact that not all critics of economics are journalists; they include insiders – academic economists who dissent from the views that dominate the profession.

A very recent example is *Economics Confronts the Economy* (2006) in which Philip Klein argued that most economists were involved in peddling an unchanging *laissez-faire* view of the world. The face of economics is, he claimed, failing to change because academic economics is controlled by a comparatively small group of economists located in the top departments (University of Chicago, MIT, Stanford, Harvard and so on) who edit the leading journals and act as a barrier to the emergence of new ideas. Most research in the subject, Klein argues, is characterized by the trivialization of the subject and a search for elegance, irrespective of the costs. If we look elsewhere, we find *A Guide to What's Wrong with Economics* (Fullbrook 2004) in which no fewer than twenty-seven authors wrote about different and allegedly fundamental flaws in the subject. Or Steven Marglin's *Dismal Science: How Thinking Like an Economist Undermines Community* (2008), the message of which is clear from its title. These books echo the views of many heterodox economists, who are convinced that most of their orthodox colleagues are taking the subject down the wrong path.

So why is it that intelligent, seemingly well-informed economists can have such different views of their subject? To put it another way, how can one economist take the view that the discipline is successfully solving the problems confronting society, whilst another sees the discipline as engaging in abstract theorizing that has no bearing on the real world? These are questions that need to be answered if we are to make sense of modern economics.

To place this discussion in context, it is important to be clear that
these questions are not unique to economics. Of course, economics does
exhibit more disagreement than the natural sciences. Physicists may
question whether or not the universe started with a 'big bang' or disagree
over how to explain gravity, and biologists may disagree over specific
processes of evolution. This says no more than that there are unanswered
questions in science. But such disputes are conducted within a generally accepted framework: the laws of physics cannot simply be rejected
(though they may periodically be seen in a new light), and within biology
the principle of evolution through natural selection is not questioned,
though the manner of its operation may be debated. But in the social
sciences, fundamental disagreements exist and remain unresolved. The
complexity of the problems that are dealt with in the social sciences and
the way human societies are continually evolving, developing new institutions within which people interact in different ways means that the
social sciences probably never will possess empirical bases that are as
firm as those on which the natural sciences rest.

Even so, economics is unusual. The field has had a much stronger disciplinary identity than most other social sciences, with greater agreement on what the core of the subject comprises. In this, it is closer to
the natural sciences than it is to, for example, psychology, its great rival
within the social sciences. Psychology has what has been described as a
'protean identity': it is a 'trans-discipline' that encompasses approaches
that are as hard to reconcile as behaviourism and psychoanalysis and in
which there is no agreement on something as basic (to an outsider) as
whether 'the mind' is even a meaningful concept. Sociology, too, despite
the claims of those who see it as the master social science, is so varied
that one can question whether it is even possible to speak of a single
sociology rather than many sociologies. Similarly, political science comprises disciplines (political theory, political behaviour and international
relations) between which there are clear divides.

But economics' strong disciplinary identity does not translate into
agreement like that found in the natural sciences, for there remain economists who dissent from what, in the eyes of most of their colleagues, are
basic presuppositions that all economists should accept. In some cases
this goes sufficiently far that dissenters effectively cease to communicate

with other economists, creating communities that advocate alternative heterodox approaches to the subject. Thus, when the credit crunch called into question the conventional wisdom on the benefits of deregulated financial markets, there were groups that had always been sceptical about the stability of unregulated markets; they stood ready to claim that their views of the world had been vindicated.

THE PROSECUTION

A clear example of recent disquiet with economics is the movement known as Post-Autistic Economics, which was started in June 2000, when a group of students at École normale supérieure, in Paris, published a petition protesting the state of economics and the way it was taught. They claimed that economics had come to be concerned only with imaginary worlds, that mathematical techniques had become an end in themselves, and that the teaching of economics had become excessively dogmatic.

Most of us have chosen to study economics so as to acquire a deep understanding of economic phenomena with which the citizens of today are confronted. But the teaching that is offered, that is to say for the most part neoclassical theory or approaches derived from it, does not generally answer this expectation. Indeed, even when the theory legitimately detaches itself from contingencies in the first instance, it rarely carries out the necessary return to the facts. The empirical side (historical facts, functioning of institutions, study of the behaviours and strategies of agents …) is almost non-existent. Furthermore, this gap in the teaching, this disregard for concrete realities, poses an enormous problem for those who would like to render themselves useful to economic and social actors. (Fullbrook 2004, p. 2)

This protest provoked strong reactions. A group of French economics teachers produced their own petition, echoing the students' call for greater pluralism in the teaching of the subject: teaching had become divorced from reality and the way to put this right was to broaden the curriculum. Only a more pluralistic economics would foster critical thinking and enable students to question the unthinking use of mathematics in economics. The issue became public on 21 June, when *Le Monde* published a symposium in which several economists supported the students' claims. The French education minister became involved, commissioning a report on the state of economics education in France.

The debate was not confined to France. Prominent American economists became involved in the French debate, some defending the status quo. The following June, a group of Ph.D. students at the University of Cambridge circulated a petition criticizing the narrowness of economics and calling for a debate over its foundations. They collected hundreds of signatures from academic economists in a wide variety of countries. Making use of the Internet, and taking up a phrase used in the original French students' petition, the Post-Autistic Economics Network was set up to ensure that the debate continued. Autism was used as a metaphor for the way economics had lost its sense of perspective, emphasizing one approach to the exclusion of others and not relating to the real world in any meaningful way.

If it were an isolated event, the flurry of debate over Post-Autistic Economics would not be very significant. A few hundred signatures may sound like a large number, but they represent no more than a tiny fraction of the total number of economists in the world (the American Economic Association alone has more than 20,000 members) and even of those studying economics in France. It is safe to say that, for the bulk of the profession, it was not a significant issue even after they heard about it. Most economists will have agreed with the reaction of Robert Solow, professor at MIT and winner of the Nobel Memorial Prize in Economic Science for his work on growth theory, who is widely regarded as open-minded – just the sort of economist one might expect to sympathize with the students' call for greater pluralism – that these criticisms were misconceived. He argued in *Le Monde* (3 January 2001) that any alternative theory worth taking seriously must obey the rules of logic, take account of the facts and be parsimonious, and that he could not think of a single 'alternative approach' that met these criteria. It was wrong, Solow claimed, to argue that valuable alternative approaches were being pushed aside: the dominance of American economics, to which the French students had objected, arose simply because of the size and competitiveness of the U.S. academic system.

But the French students' complaint was not an isolated event. In 2003 a group of students at Harvard argued a similar case, wanting a curriculum that would be more critical of conventional ways of thinking. Disquiet about the content of Ph.D. programmes was not confined to students. In the late 1980s there had been concern with the content of American Ph.D. programmes, prompted by a survey that found that students were highly cynical about what they were studying and that there was a widely held belief among doctoral students that many of those trained in top graduate programmes did not have a sufficiently broad education to teach undergraduates in liberal arts colleges. The problem was that graduate students in economics learned advanced mathematical techniques and could prove theorems, but they knew nothing about economic institutions, economic statistics or the issues involved in policy making. Proficiency in mathematics and the ability to solve puzzles were considered far more important to making it through graduate programmes in economics than knowing anything about the economy. Success involved being good at playing intellectual games, irrespective of whether they revealed anything about the real world. The result was that the American Economic Association established a Commission on Graduate Education in Economics (COGEE) that produced a report recommending a series of changes, though little changed as a result.

The view that the economics curriculum has become excessively narrow and places excessive emphasis on mathematical technique is held by a wide variety of economists. Some do not object to the use of mathematical theory per se – they merely want to encourage a broader, more open-minded approach to the subject. For them, the metaphor of autism suggests merely that there has been a loss of perspective – that the discipline has got its priorities wrong. They do technical work that is published in the leading journals and work alongside colleagues who are entirely happy with the status quo, and they are merely arguing for a change in direction.

However, there are others who go much further in their criticisms. These are heterodox economists whose identity as economists rests on standing out against the orthodoxy that dominates the discipline. That orthodoxy may sometimes be defined in terms of specific beliefs about the economy; more often, it is defined as hostility to the methods that are used to justify such policies. A good example of such a wholesale rejection of commonly accepted methods and practices can be found in

the book *Economics and Reality* (1997) by Tony Lawson. He argued that
orthodox economic theory and the statistical methods used to apply that
theory to real-world data are deeply flawed, being relevant only to a world
that exhibits stable empirical regularities. Such regularities, he claims, are
simply not to be found in economic phenomena, rendering the whole
enterprise fruitless. His rejection of mainstream economics was so decisive that accommodation was clearly impossible: most economists were
bound to reject the book out of hand, and it was inevitable that it would
appeal only to a minority. However, the book clearly struck a chord with
journalists and some academics, both inside and outside economics. For
many, the title said it all – economics was widely perceived as having lost
touch with reality, and the book faced up to this. Ormerod's *The Death
of Economics* (1994) got a similar response. Echoing the title of a West
End show, the line 'No reality please, we're economists' was used as the
title of a number of critical pieces about economics. Scepticism about
economics runs deep.

Heterodox economists often find inspiration in figures from the past,
looking back to economists such as Karl Marx, John Maynard Keynes,
Thorstein Veblen (the late-nineteenth-century critic of America's 'leisure class' or the late-nineteenth-century Austrians who defended the
free-market economy against its Marxist critics). What these heterodox
economists have in common is that none of them engage in modern,
technical economics. In each case, they claim that orthodox economics
has failed to see the full significance of their favoured economists' ideas.
For example, Post-Keynesians argue that, although orthodox economists
learned something from Keynes, they failed to see the significance of
what he wrote about fundamental uncertainty (i.e., uncertain events to
which it is impossible to attach meaningful numerical probabilities) and
that this failure fatally undermines orthodox theory. Other heterodox
economists are driven by specific concerns. For the Union for Radical
Political Economy these concerns are overtly political: orthodoxy fails
to take account of class, power and income distribution. Feminist economics points to hidden, gendered, presuppositions in orthodox theory,
aiming for an economics that is free of such biases.

All disciplines attract criticism from dissenters whom few practitioners take seriously. It is enough to list supporters of 'alternative' medical

therapies such as homeopathy; creationists who espouse 'intelligent design' as an alternative to evolution; parapsychologists and astrologers. In most cases they can be dismissed as cranks. Peer reviewing in academic journals is, after all, about ensuring that only respectable work gets published, and professional qualifications are about excluding those who do not follow accepted practices in fields such as medicine or psychology. Heterodox economists may feel that their place in the profession is tenuous, a view that is borne out by the widespread ignorance of their work. But heterodoxy is a phenomenon that has been around a long time.

THE DEFENCE

Most critics write from the belief that economics is dominated by an orthodoxy that prescribes the use of a particular, highly abstract theory and a tightly circumscribed range of methods that together serve to exclude serious treatment of real-world problems. The normal response is that, even if it were once correct, this characterization is so out of date as to amount to a caricature of what is going on in the field. It may have been the case in, say, the 1960s, or even the 1980s, but there has also been such a proliferation of radically new approaches to economics that the charge of methodological narrowness is impossible to sustain. If there is a central theoretical framework for the subject, it is game theory, which can be used to analyse issues of strategy and power, not the theory of general competitive equilibrium on which critics often focus. Furthermore, because game theory yields results that are highly sensitive to context, it forces economists to pay attention to institutional details. Such details might include the procedures according to which wage bargaining is conducted, the remuneration packages received by managers, the barriers to establishing new firms, or the use of anti-competitive practices.

Not only that, but economists have been able to use their 'excessively abstract' theories to help create markets where none previously existed. When John McMillan, a New Zealander whose career at Stanford ended with his untimely death in 2007, who specialized in the theory of auctions, wrote *Reinventing the Bazaar* (2002), he had in mind a phenomenon that was not just the result of politicians being willing to consider

market solutions to economic problems but also the result of economists'
applying their theories to real-world problems. Theory made it possible
to establish where markets could be made to work and how they should
be designed. Similarly, critics were for a long time sceptical about 'experimental economics' in which human subjects have to make decisions in a
controlled environment with a researcher monitoring their actions. But
such experiments, like game theory, have been used to help design new
markets and to solve real-world problems.

Economics has also become much more empirical than its critics
imply. Looking at the U.S. academic job market in 2007, Angus Deaton, a
Princeton professor who was involved in the university's hiring process,
observed that it had become normal for Ph.D. students looking for jobs
to offer papers based on extensive empirical work, the result of searching through large data sets (*RES Newsletter* April 2007, p. 5). Topics he
encountered included the prison parole system in Georgia, HIV/AIDS in
Africa, child immunization in India, political bias in newspapers, child
soldiers, racial profiling, leisure choices, mosquito nets, treating leukae-
mia, child development, and the relationships to each other of war, television, bilingualism and democracy. This list is given in full to show its
variety. Furthermore, few of these, Deaton claimed, relied substantially
on either economic theory or the most advanced econometric (statistical) techniques. Most of the job candidates he encountered were weak on
traditional price theory but possessed considerable data-handling skills.

One of the best illustrations of the changes that have taken place in
economics is the theory of finance. During the 1980s and 1990s, evidence accumulated that rational behaviour could not explain fluctuations in stock market prices: prices fluctuated much more than could be
explained by the 'fundamentals', such as corporate profits, that should
have explained them if investors were rational. To explain this, economists turned to psychology. Investors might assume that past trends
would continue, investing in stocks whose prices had risen; they might
attribute successful investments to their own skill, whilst blaming unsuc-
cessful ones on bad luck; or they might hold on to some stocks too long,
because taking losses was so painful. Stories may begin to circulate
about why certain stocks are doing well (perhaps due to the emergence
of a 'new economy' or new sources of profit via the Internet), apparently

verified by rising stock prices, causing a speculative bubble to develop. All of this could be used to help explain what was termed 'excess volatility'. To test such psychological or 'behavioural' explanations, economists constructed experiments: they had human subjects in laboratories taking investment decisions (for real money, even if their possible rewards and losses were less than they might have got on the real stock exchange) under controlled conditions. Economists also looked hard for 'natural experiments', such as dramatic booms and collapses in countries with weak regulatory regimes, such as Albania in 1996–7.

HOW CAN THEY SEE THE SUBJECT SO DIFFERENTLY?

How is it that supporters can see economics as engaging with the real world, providing the tools that enable economists to solve fundamental problems and guide policy, whilst critics see it as arid mathematical formalism that either has no practical implications or is positively harmful?

One possible answer is that people are looking at different things. Defenders of the subject naturally look at the best examples, for that is what matters given that once research is in the public domain people can select the best and ignore substandard work. After all, few would wish to judge science by the research highlighted in the *Journal of Irreproducible Results* or the *Annals of Improbable Research*. Critics, on the other hand, may be focusing on the 'average' piece of academic research, or even responding to the larger quantity of unimaginative, routine work that is of much less value. Economics is so vast, that by looking in different places it is possible to see very different things: the articles in the *Journal of Economic Theory* or the *Journal of Mathematical Economics*, for example, are typically more mathematical and more abstract – less obviously related to the real world – than those in *American Economic Review*, let alone the *Brookings Papers on Economic Activity* or journals in applied fields. Articles that one journal would reject as unsuitable for its readership are often welcomed by a different journal. However, whilst economics is extremely diverse and many economists have become specialists in comparatively narrow fields, this is not the whole story: there has to be a reason why economists cannot see outside their own field. Moreover, it would not explain why different economists have very different standards of what constitutes a persuasive argument: for some economists, it is theoretical arguments that are ultimately persuasive; for others, theory that is not backed up by statistical evidence is unpersuasive.

Another dimension to the problem is the difference between research and teaching. Some critics focus on economics teaching (this was the original complaint of the Paris students and what underlay the COGEE report discussed earlier in this chapter), but those who defend the vitality of modern economics focus on the latest research. It would be no surprise to find a lag between research findings and academic curriculum – indeed, it could hardly be otherwise. Diane Coyle, one of the defenders of modern economics, has appealed to teachers to update their curricula, so that potential graduate students are not turned away from economics by being exposed to theories that convey none of the excitement that is found in the latest economic research (*RES Newsletter* April 2007, p. 10). But again, this cannot be the complete explanation: not only do many critics focus on research and topics that do not appear in any but the most advanced curricula, but it also begs the question of why there is such a chasm between teaching and research. There will be some lags, but nothing that can explain why perceptions differ so much.

A further possibility is that some economists judge economics solely by its policy relevance, whereas others see it as a 'purer' science. There are undoubtedly differences here, but they fail to capture the contrast between orthodox and heterodox views. They do lead to the question of when and how economists decide that it is justifiable to draw policy conclusions from their analyses. Again, policy relevance versus pure science may be part of the story, but it does not fully answer the question, for it begs the question of how there could be such differing view of what economics involves without economists themselves being aware of it. Physical geography and human geography are radically different subjects and may be a source of friction to the extent that their cohabitation under the label 'geography' can sometimes be difficult; yet this disparity does not cause confusion in the field. Neither does the range of types of psychology or sociology. There is something peculiar about economics.

It is also possible that the difference might be ideological. One of the characteristics of heterodox economic groups is that many of them are associated with a particular political position. Austrian economists, a school of economic thought that traces its ancestry back to economists based in late-nineteenth century Vienna, are clearly committed to free markets and are generally hostile to the state for reasons that are political as much as economic. Radicals, Post-Keynesians, old-style Institutionalists and Marxists envisage a substantial role for the state. In contrast, though orthodox economists clearly have ideological positions (it could not be otherwise), and though economists are probably on average politically to the right of other social scientists, their groupings are, at least not ostensibly, premised on any political beliefs. And yet, the outrage expressed by some orthodox economists at any questioning of central doctrines does suggest that ideology may be more significant than their claims to being 'scientific' may suggest. Why else would economists have reacted so strongly to the widely reported finding by David Card and Alan Krueger in the mid-1990s that imposing a minimum wage in New Jersey had not raised unemployment compared with neighbouring Pennsylvania, where there was no minimum wage, and it might even have reduced it? The evidence may have been open to question, but so too is much of the empirical work that is regularly published in leading journals, and it does not elicit anything like the same degree of criticism. Moreover, the finding that any effect was small should not have been surprising in that economists have been trying, and failing, for decades to find a relationship between minimum wages and unemployment. Why else would mainstream economists liken any attack on free trade to astrology as something that does not merit being taken seriously, given that the imposition of free trade, even if beneficial in the long run, usually has costs that need to be weighed against the benefits?

Or is it simply, as many orthodox economists maintain, that those who question what is going on in economics simply cannot understand what is going on, often because they have never developed the necessary technical skills? Heterodox economists, they claim, do not even read the most up-to-date literature and persist in doing economics in an old-fashioned way. On the other hand, perhaps orthodox economists are simply so committed to the tools they have invested so much time in learning that they cannot afford to take a broader view of what is going on in their subject? But in both cases it is easy to point to exceptions that make such simple answers problematic. There are orthodox economists whose knowledge and sympathies cause them to look beyond the confines of economic theory, drawing on history, sociology, psychology and philosophy to create complex explanations that go beyond any orthodox paradigm. And there are heterodox economists whose command of technical material would enable them, if they chose, to work along more orthodox lines.

SOLVING THE PUZZLE

Is economics the most rigorous of the social sciences, then, or little more than the expression of a free-market ideology? And is there something about the discipline that explains the persistence of such contrasting views of what it can achieve? To answer such questions, the best place to start is with some examples, to see what happens when economists use their ideas to tackle problems of economic policy. The reason for this is not to divert attention from the abstract theories attacked by critics; it is because this is where we would expect to find evidence about what economics can and cannot do. Chapters 2 to 5, therefore, explore a range of case studies, from controlling sulphur dioxide emissions to the Russian transition to capitalism to recent monetary policy. These case studies have been chosen because they illustrate the discipline's strengths and weaknesses. Chapters 6 to 9 then offer a historical perspective on the body of ideas and techniques that make up economics today. The reason for offering this perspective is to try to make sense of the variety of approaches found within economics today by looking at the ways economic theory has been shaped by economists' attempts to make their discipline scientific, and to tackle the questions of ideology and dissent head-on. These problems are both ones where the key lies in what has happened in the discipline since the Second World War. These themes are then brought together in Chapter 10, which tries to make sense of modern economics, avoiding the Scylla of uncritical praise and the Charybdis of denunciation, by reflecting on the different ways in which economic knowledge is created and the relationship between economic science and the creation and criticism of economic myths.

PART I

ECONOMICS IN ACTION

If we are to understand the state of modern economics, we need to tackle the problem of economic theory. For, more than any other social science, economics is dominated by modelling. Economic theory typically involves the working out of the implications of rational choice in a variety of contexts. This may be done using mathematics, or it may just involve logical analysis, expressed in everyday language. Similarly, empirical (or applied) work typically involves the construction of models that differ from theoretical ones in that they contain numbers that are derived from statistical data. Enthusiasts for modern economics and its critics are in complete agreement that modelling is central to the subject as it exists today. What they disagree on is whether these theories tell us much that is useful about the world.

Take the genre of 'economics explains everything' books, cited at the start of Chapter 1. Much of this literature is based on analysing data to find paradoxical results, such as links between abortion and crime or patterns in baby naming. There contain little formal theory, let alone mathematics, but these books demonstrate the power of economics by showing how empirical results can be explained by assuming that people behave rationally in the circumstances they face. The message is that simple ideas explain a lot of different things. On the other side, critics

claim that the problem with economics is that viewing people as rational optimizers involves accepting an impoverished, one-dimensional
account of human behaviour. Each side is looking at the same theory but
drawing an opposite conclusion.

The best way to tackle this problem is not the obvious one, that is, by
starting with abstract economic theory; it is to start with what happens
when economics is used to solve practical problems. The value of economic theory and of the methods that economists have developed for
using their theories depends on what happens when theory is applied
to real-world problems. The four chapters in Part II are chosen, not
because they provide a comprehensive account of what economists do,
but because they provide a representative sample of important problems
tackled by economists. They also illustrate particularly clearly the circumstances in which economics appears to work and in which it appears
not to work.

The conclusion that emerges from these chapters is that, where problems are narrowly and precisely defined, and where they involve agents
whose motivations are well understood and who operate under well-understood constraints, economic analysis is remarkably powerful. Though
it has not always been so, finance is often thought to be the paradigm
case where theories of rational or profit-maximizing choice apply. Agents
are professional, informed traders, their objectives comprising clearly
defined variables such as the return on their portfolios and the risk to
which they are exposed. The volume of transactions is sufficiently high
and markets are sufficiently well organized according to well-understood
rules that the constraints they face are clear. In finance, economists can
claim great success: Fischer Black and his associates, discussed in Chapter 6, had a vision of the world that they wanted to create, and they were
able to create it. Reality was made to conform to theory. Of course, the
2008 crisis showed that there were problems, but this does not undermine the claim that, within a limited sphere, the theory of finance was
highly successful. Similar remarks could be made about the U.S. acid
rain program and the U.K. third-generation (3G) telecommunications
spectrum auction, discussed in Chapter 3. The agents involved were professionals with clearly defined objectives. When confronted with a clear
set of rules, they behaved in the way that economists had predicted, with

the result that policy makers achieved the outcomes they desired. In the case of the U.S. acid rain program, they even managed to design a system that was able to cope with unexpected events.

Economics works best when objectives are precisely defined and, hardly surprising, when people behave in ways that correspond to the assumptions made in economic theory. However, something that emerges from these examples is worth repeating: success arose, at least in part, from the *creation* of circumstances under which economic theories worked. The best example is financial markets. Prior to the development of the economic theories discussed in Chapter 5, financial markets did not resemble the 'perfect' markets central to economic theory; there were numerous regulations and legal barriers to certain types of transactions. But economic ideas played a significant role in persuading people to make the changes that enabled the creation of new markets. Economic theories were, to use a term favoured by some sociologists, performative: the use of certain theories led to the creation of a world where the theories were applicable.

However, when a broader picture is considered, the complications begin to become apparent. The 3G telecommunications auction had unintended consequences for the structure of the industry. The establishment of hedge funds, discussed in Chapter 6, made it possible for informed investors to reap great rewards, but it may have had harmful effects on others, even bringing about financial crises that were wholly unintended: the development of new financial products may have benefited those who understood them and were able to take advantage of them, but the consequences for many other people were disastrous. Inflation targeting, also discussed in Chapter 6, appeared to have been successful in promoting stability for about a decade after its introduction, though the broader effects of the policy were harder to judge. The sub-prime mortgage crisis that emerged in 2007 and the subsequent recession reinforced some of those doubts. The main lesson from these various case studies is that, when judging success or failure, very careful attention needs to be paid to the criteria that are being used. In all of these cases, when the results of applying economic ideas are judged against relatively narrow criteria, economics appears to have had great successes; but that when wider ramifications are considered things become less clear.

The limitations of economic analysis emerge far more starkly in the case of the Soviet transition from socialism to capitalism, discussed in Chapter 4. When an entire society is being transformed, it becomes impossible to separate the economic from the social and political. The failure to implement a less catastrophic transition (and any transition that reduces life expectancy by a decade can only be described as catastrophic) may mean that the economic theories on which it was based were fundamentally flawed, but it could equally reflect a situation in which it was impossible to manage the transition. Soviet society was collapsing so quickly that the options for preventing it from descending into chaos were severely limited, and the path that was followed was perhaps as good as it could have been, whatever economic advice had been taken.

However, whilst a rapid transition may have been inevitable, this does not vindicate the economists who supported it. Where economists appear to have gone wrong was in their failure to see how existing Soviet society worked and, as a result, what the effects of deregulation and privatization would be. Opportunities for profit could be, and were, found in manipulating the system as much as in productive activities – after all, during the Soviet era, people had learned how to work the system. The Soviet experience of transformation shows that a market economy requires much more than freedom from government intervention to run smoothly. It requires an elaborate structure of institutions where the term is interpreted very broadly to include not just property rights and the infrastructure required for markets to exist but also appropriate habits of mind. Furthermore, understanding what happened in Russia involves venturing outside economics, for these events revealed how economic developments were intertwined with features of Russian society and politics.

Similar conclusions can be drawn from discussions of globalization, discussed in Chapter 5. Economic theory has very powerful techniques for analysing the effects of a narrow range of motives within tightly defined sets of institutions, but when considering the transformation of an entire society, attention must be paid to a broader range of human motivations and to institutions that are not within the control of policy makers. Psychology and sociology also need to be involved. Economists are developing theories to deal with some of these broader problems, but they remain limited in scope. Generally, economists' theories identify mechanisms that might be operating rather than provide a very general theory of what is going on in society as a whole. Theories of the economy as a whole, whether general equilibrium theories dealing with the interaction of large numbers of firms and households or macroeconomic theories dealing with aggregates, rarely take account of these institutional details because the resulting systems would be too difficult to specify completely, let alone to solve, even if there was agreement on the approach that should be taken. Because the problems are so broad, the available theory and evidence leave much scope for the intrusion of both intellectual values and ideology.

2

Creating New Markets

ECONOMISTS AND MARKETS

Economists have always been concerned with markets. For the most part, they have been concerned with how markets operated – whether they were competitive or monopolistic and whether they needed to be regulated. There might even be products (such as one where technology meant that monopoly would emerge naturally or where it might be wasteful to have more than one supplier) that could better be provided by the state than through markets. However, it was generally accepted that some goods could be bought and sold in markets but others could not. Thus, whilst there could be markets for rice, motor vehicles, fuel or water, it was not possible to have a market for 'goods' such as clean air. Government provision and regulation were required to achieve social objectives.

In the closing decades of the twentieth century economists began to challenge this consensus: they have, to use a phrase cited in Chapter 1, reinvented the bazaar. A literature developed on the operation of government and bureaucracies that pointed out that governments, as well as markets, could fail. Critics of government action were able to point to many examples where government allocation of resources appeared to be highly inefficient. In response, economists argued for extending the scope of markets. Here, we consider two examples, first, the creation of markets in the United States to combat the problem of acid rain caused by sulphur dioxide emissions, and second, the creation of a market for the part of the radio frequency spectrum set aside for third-generation

(3G) mobile phone networks. The latter focuses on the UK spectrum auction, though similar remarks could be made about the equivalent U.S. auction in the 1990s.

THE U.S. ACID RAIN PROGRAM

In 1990, President George H. W. Bush signed Title IV of the Clean Air Act Amendments. This act established a system of tradable emission permits to control the level of sulphur dioxide emissions from electricity-generation plants. The idea of creating a market to solve an environmental problem came from economists, who are trained to think of all decisions in terms of balancing marginal costs and benefits. Many non-economists were hostile to the idea, preferring regulation. One prominent environmental economist went so far as to argue,

> In the early days of 'Environmental Regulation' in the late 1960s and early 1970s, the role of economic analysis in the design and implementation of policies for protection of the environment was viewed with suspicion, and in some instances with outright hostility, by many environmentalists. Economic forces were seen by many as the basic source of environmental degradation, and effective policy had to combat these forces, not cooperate with them. Much of the early legislation embodied this perspective. In the United States, for example, the Clean Air Act of 1970 forbade the use of benefit-cost analysis in the determination of standards for environmental quality. Such standards were to be set to protect the public health without regard to costs of attainment. (Oates 1992, p. xiii)

The emergence of a market solution to an environmental problem thus owed much to economists working on the idea.

Acid rain arises from the emission of sulphur dioxide (SO_2) and various nitrogen oxides (nitric oxide and nitrous oxide, generally referred to as NO_x, short for NO, NO_2 and N_2O) into the atmosphere. When these chemicals dissolve in water they form sulphuric and nitric acid, which falls in rain, with damaging effects on the environment and human health. In the 1970s, the main concern was with the effects of SO_2 and atmospheric sulphuric acid on human health, but by about 1980 concern about the environmental effects had increased. In the United States the main cause of acid rain was the production of SO_2 as a by-product of electricity generation, especially in coal-burning power stations. Given that electricity must be generated, the issue becomes one of reducing the level of emissions per unit of heat (measured in BTUs [British thermal units]) produced (or per kilowatt hour of electricity generated). This reduction can be achieved in two ways. One is to equip power stations with air filters called 'scrubbers', which filter waste gases as they go up the stacks, removing SO_2. The other is to burn coal that has lower sulphur content. But both of these options are costly, which means that companies, whose only concern is profit, will not implement them unless they are either required to do so or are given an incentive to do so.

An important complication is that the cost of reducing emissions varies greatly from plant to plant and region to region. The key factor is access to different grades of coal. Some power stations could easily switch from high- to low-sulphur coal and could reduce emissions very cheaply. For others, the switch to low-sulphur coal would mean getting it from much farther away and paying higher transport costs. The cost of installing scrubbers was high, and their effect on emissions depended on the kind of coal being burned: they were efficient only if high-sulphur coal was being burned, and switching to low-sulphur coal is expensive.

During the 1970s, the U.S. government had tried to control emissions through regulation. An amendment to the Clean Air Act passed in 1970 had specified, among other measures, that new coal-fired power stations could not emit more than 1.2 pounds of sulphur dioxide per million BTU of heat generated. It was assumed that this would gradually reduce overall emissions as older power stations were retired. The level of 1.2 lb/m BTU for new units was technically feasible. But the policy did not work. The regulation gave companies an incentive to extend the life of older and dirtier power stations, which were not subject to these restrictions, and they had no incentive to raise efficiency of existing plants, whether they were operating above or below the threshold. Many states failed to meet their obligations, and in 1977 the regulations were amended. Regions not meeting their obligations were subject to further controls, and new regulations were introduced to prevent utilities that were below their 1.2 lb/m BTU target from meeting additional demand by burning cheaper high-sulphur coal (which they could do without exceeding their limits).

The new standards required that all new coal-fired plants be fitted with scrubbers, which removed the incentive to use low-sulphur coal.

Another problem was the way the new regulations affected different regions. Because of the prevailing winds and the distribution of the industry across the United States, acid rain, which by 1980 was emerging as an environmental problem, affected the northeastern states more than others. Western states were less affected by acid rain and concerned about having to incur the high cost of installing scrubbers in all new power stations to clean up their already clean emissions. The uneven distribution of coal stocks was also important. The main high-sulphur coal producers were in the East, in Appalachia, and they opposed acid rain controls. Western states, with easier access to low-sulphur coal, opposed measures that would give advantages to eastern producers of high-sulphur coal. Midwestern industrial states, containing many of the most polluting power stations, opposed measures that would significantly raise their production costs. Thus, not only did the complexity of the situation make it virtually impossible to design workable regulations, even if an efficient regulatory solution could be found, but such regulations were also unlikely to attract sufficient political support to be viable. The prospects for significant reduction in acid rain levels seemed remote.

The regulatory framework was changed in a 1990 Amendment to the Clean Air Act that amended the previous amendment. The target was to reduce emissions from the 1980 levels of 19 million tons per year to 9 million tons per year by 2000, a reduction of 10 million tons. This shift was to be achieved in two phases. In the first, from 1995 to 1999, the 263 dirtiest large power plants were required to reduce emissions by 3.5 million tons per year. In phase two, almost all fossil-fuelled generating plants were subject to the national ceiling. These limits were translated (using a complicated formula, the result of intense political bargaining) into allowable emissions for each operator. Operators would then be given permits (each of which allows its holder to emit one ton of SO_2 in the given year) for these amounts. These permits could be bought and sold freely, and they could be 'banked' for future use.

This changed the nature of the decision that facing producers had to make. Because permits could be bought and sold, generators that could reduce pollution cheaply could cut emissions and sell the permits they did not need, and those for whom reductions were more expensive could buy permits. To ensure that a market for permits did emerge, the federal Environmental Protection Agency (EPA) retained a small proportion of permits, which they planned to sell at periodic auctions. The proceeds would be paid to the producers from whose allowances they had been taken. Competition would keep the price of permits sufficiently high as to induce producers to cut emissions to the required level. Pollution would be cut to the required level in the most efficient way possible.

There was considerable fear that a well-functioning market would not emerge. For example, one concern was that firms would not be confident that the regime would continue unchanged and would take the precaution of holding on to surplus permits, and that firms wanting to buy permits would be unable to do so. Early on, it was forecast that in phase 1 the price of permits would range from $290 to $410 and that in phase 2 it would increase to $580 to $815. In relation to the costs of generating electricity, these sums were very high. However, these fears turned out to be unfounded. A market developed rapidly, with the price of permits around $150.

As phase I got under way, the price of permits fell to $65 in early 1996, after which it rose, by the end of 1998, to about $200. From about 1994 on, prices were quoted regularly. There was also a significant volume of trading activity. By March 1998, the number of permits that had been sold in the EPA auctions had reached 1.3 million. This was a small number compared to the 20.3 million permits that were traded privately. Operators that emitted more SO_2 than their allocation were buying permits from the large number of operators that had managed to reduce emissions more than they were required to do. Futures markets in permits developed, and prices in these suggested that producers were not particularly fearful of being caught short: they had confidence that they would be able to buy permits should they turn out to need them.

The policy appeared to work in that targets were achieved, and there was complete compliance: firms either reduced emissions or purchased the necessary permits. There was no need to make exemptions or to amend the rules. Estimating the precise effects of Title IV is difficult, because emissions had been falling before it came into effect, in part because deregulation and increased competition in the railroad business caused the price of low-sulphur coal in the East to fall. This made it more attractive, even without any environmental regulations, for Eastern and Midwestern generators to switch to low-sulphur coal, reducing their emissions. There were also some contracts to install scrubbers already in the pipeline before Title IV came into effect. Still, it seems clear that the new emissions targets would not have been met without the new system of regulation.

The new system also appears to have encouraged innovation and changes in production methods that reduced the cost of cutting SO_2 emissions. The cost of installing scrubbers, though still high, came down. Methods were developed to overcome the technical problems associated with converting furnaces from high-sulphur coal to low-sulphur coal (which typically produces more ash and water): producers experimented with mixtures of the two types of coal until they found the most efficient one. Producers in regions where switching to low-sulphur coal was prohibitively expensive did not automatically install expensive scrubbers, but often switched to using medium-sulphur coal, and new sources of supply emerged, with some coal mines altering the type of coal they produced. The premium for low-sulphur coal, which had fluctuated greatly during the 1980s, settled down from the beginning of 1994 to a level that, when adjusted appropriately, was very close to the price of permits. This outcome was consistent with what one would expect to observe if resources were being allocated efficiently. Adjustment to the new regime was not perfect, but it coped with unexpected surprises. The main one was the effect of railroad deregulation. Because low-sulphur coal became cheaper, the Midwest found it easier than expected to meet emission requirements. However, though the price of permits did not initially reflect the costs of reducing emissions, the adjustment did not create major problems. In particular, the fact that permits could readily be bought meant that it was impossible for particular producers to argue that they needed to be exempted from meeting their obligations, as typically happened under conventional forms of regulation.

The problem of reducing SO_2 emissions in the United States exhibited certain features that made it possible for a market solution to work much as economics textbooks suggested it should. The number of firms that had to be monitored was limited, and meters could be installed in flues to monitor emissions. This made it possible to strictly enforce emissions, but it avoided the problems that would have arisen had inspectors had to monitor practices inside the plants. It was possible to set targets in terms of total emissions, not in terms of reductions, which would have been much harder to measure because of the difficulty in defining a baseline. It also helped that, compared with, for example, the cost of reducing CO_2 emissions, the industries affected were relatively small in relation to total U.S. production. Questions of income distribution did arise, notably among regions and among various groups of producers, but these issues were minor compared with what could arise in other contexts (such as global warming).

The ideas of creating property rights in the form of permits to pollute and achieving an optimal allocation through organizing a competitive market are clearly associated with economists. Noneconomists are often sceptical about such schemes, believing that simpler regulations will be fairer and more effective. However, whether or not Title IV was the best possible scheme, it can legitimately be described as a success. It was more successful than the previous regime because certain features of the electricity generation industry in the United States made it impossible to design effective 'command-and-control' regulations and at the same time made it possible for a market in pollution permits to work.

THE BRITISH 3G TELECOM AUCTION

On 27 April 2000, the British government concluded an auction in which they sold licenses to operate the third-generation (3G) mobile phone networks – on which subscribers would have high-speed Internet access over their mobile phones. The government had expected the auction to raise £3–4 billion, but the outcome was £22.5 billion (35.53 billion USD or 39 billion Euros). The auction design had been the outcome of three years' preparation, in which advice from economists (Paul Klemperer at Oxford and Ken Binmore at University College London) had been decisive. From the government's point of view, and that of its advisers, it was clearly an example of the successful use of economics.

The government was faced with the problem of creating licenses and then allocating them to private companies that would construct the 3G networks in such a way as to best meet objectives. The objectives that eventually emerged were (1) to assign the spectrum efficiently; (2) to promote competition; and (3) to 'realize the full economic value' (subject to the other two objectives). Efficiency meant that the available radio spectrum should be allocated to the companies to whom it was worth most. Competition required having several networks and provided a limit on the revenue that could be raised, because revenue would be maximized by giving one firm a monopoly that would allow it to charge very high prices. Though they were apparently straightforward, these objectives took time to evolve. There were also constraints imposed by technology (for example, bandwidths could not be too small).

The first decision involved how the licenses were to be created. There were several possibilities. One was to sell the radio spectrum in a large number of small pieces and allow the phone companies to purchase as many as they wished to create the bandwidths they required. The disadvantage was that this would inhibit competition, for the end result might be very few holdings or even a single large one. The decision was taken to sell a fixed number of licenses (initially four, later increased to five) and to allow firms to bid for no more than one of them. Once bought, licenses could not be combined, ensuring that the number of operators would not fall below four (or five). If a company bought a license, it committed itself to providing coverage to at least 80 per cent of the country. At this stage of the process, the emphasis was on ensuring competition.

The next decision was whether to allocate licenses through an auction or through what is often referred to as a 'beauty contest' (the government invites proposals and chooses the one that best meets its objectives). Beauty contests had often been used to choose between rival bids, but they presented problems because the criteria used were often subjective and had to be weighed against each other. (For example, in allocating a TV franchise, how does the government judge the quality of programming promised, and how is the provision of popular programmes balanced against provision of programmes that cater to minority interests?) In the case of 3G licenses, it was believed that an auction would be better. It would be simpler, more transparent and less prone to favouritism. Perhaps more important, it would be more likely to meet the first and third objectives. The reason for this conclusion is that, in order to allocate licenses efficiently, to the firms to which they were most valuable, it was necessary to find a mechanism for discovering the values firms placed on them. Because the technology was still undeveloped, there were no precedents (the United Kingdom was the first country to auction 3G rights), and there was enormous uncertainty about how much the licenses were worth. The companies concerned clearly had views on these valuations, but it was impossible for the government to consult them – they would have had an incentive to claim they were worth very little in the hope of getting them cheaply. A suitably designed auction would, it was believed, ensure that licenses went to the firms that valued them most, for they would be prepared to pay the highest prices. This would also meet the objective of raising as much revenue as possible.

It was also decided to sell the licenses for lump sums. If operators had to make royalty payments (for example, 1¢ per call made over the new networks) this cost would be likely to get passed on to consumers, and the networks would not be used efficiently. Lump-sum payments were believed not to affect the prices that operators would charge.

Once these decisions were made, the task was to design the auction in a suitable way. Two broad types of auction were considered. One is the ascending, or 'English' auction, which starts at a low price, and where bidders drop out as the price rises beyond what they are prepared to pay. The other is the 'Dutch' auction, where the price starts high and is reduced until someone bids. A variant of this is the 'sealed bid' auction, where firms submit bids, which are not opened until all bids are in. The reason auction theory, a field of economics developed during the 1980s and 1990s, is important is that the outcome of an auction can be very sensitive to how an auction is designed. The two types of auction do not in general produce the same outcome. There are several reasons that this is so.

One reason is that a successful auction requires plenty of bidders. If there are too few, there will be little competition, and those who value the asset most will not be forced to pay as much as they are prepared to pay. In the extreme case, if the number of bidders is no greater than the number of goods being sold, there is no reason for them to go above the reserve price. Given the cost of bidding for spectrum licenses, bidders would enter only if they had a realistic chance of success. Here, the problem was that potential bidders did not start on an equal footing. Four potential bidders were the existing second-generation (2G) mobile phone operators, One-2-One (which later became T-Mobile), Cellnet (later O2), Orange, and Vodafone. Because they already had radio masts installed, brand recognition and other infrastructure in place, they were at an advantage compared with new entrants. If new entrants thought they were competing head-to-head with existing operators, they would be likely to conclude that their chances of success were slim and decide not to enter the auction.

To understand this situation, it is necessary to digress briefly into auction theory. In auctions such as the 3G auction, where the value of the asset being auctioned is uncertain, each bidder has information about the asset, but no one knows the 'true' value. Some information will be available to all bidders, but each bidder will, typically, have private information that is not available to other bidders (or to the auctioneer). This means that if you and I are bidding for something, your bids provide me with useful information. If you bid $90, it tells me that you think the value is at least $90. This means that in an English auction, bidders will learn from other bidders' bids. If I know you are willing to pay $90, it may make me willing to pay $95. Even if I am not sure whether it is worth this much, the fact that you also think it is worth at least $90 reduces the chance that my information is completely wrong. In contrast, in Dutch auctions, bidders have no information about other bidders' bids, so far less information is provided by the auction.

A related problem is the so-called 'winner's curse'. This means that where the value of the asset being auctioned is uncertain, the winner typically pays more than it is worth. Suppose there are two bidders, each having different information, and that one of them overestimates the value of the asset, while the other underestimates it. The one who overestimates it will win because he or she will be prepared to pay the higher price. The problem is that he or she will discover this only after the bidding. In other words, in an English auction, if my competitor stops bidding with the result that I win the auction, I know I am likely to have gone too far. It also applies to Dutch or sealed-bid auctions. One might think that the existence of a winner's curse might not matter to the person selling the asset. The problem is that it may deter entry, or at least result in unduly cautious bidding strategies. A way around the problem is to design the auction so that the winner gets the asset, but at the second-highest price offered. That way, a bidder can bid what he or she thinks the asset is worth, knowing that if his competitors have information that means it is worth less than this, he or she will only have to pay what they value it at.

To ensure entry into the 3G auction, the number of licenses was critical. In the end, the government decided that it was feasible to auction five licenses. As this was greater than the number of incumbent firms (the four existing 2G operators), it was certain that one would go to a new entrant, providing the incentive to enter (bidding for more than one was prohibited). Initially, however, it was thought that technological constraints meant that a maximum of four licenses could be sold (otherwise bandwidth would be too small for a satisfactory service), which created a problem. The proposed solution was to hold a two-stage auction. The first stage would be an ascending auction, which would stop when the number of bidders was down one more than the number of licenses. There would then be a second stage, involving a sealed-bid auction.

Why would this arrangement encourage entry? The answer is that if the auction were a simple English auction, new entrants who start knowing that they have a disadvantage relative to incumbent firms would hesitate to bid above an incumbent. Whatever the new entrants bid, the incumbent firms would know that they could afford to bid a little higher, and would be likely always to win. New entrants stand a better chance in a sealed-bid auction, where incumbents are not able to employ the strategy of bidding slightly higher than new entrants. If the second stage were a sealed-bid auction, and one new entrant was guaranteed to enter the second stage (because five firms go through) in which they would stand a good chance of winning, newcomers might be prepared to enter.

Another potential problem with auctions is collusion between potential entrants. This might take various forms. One is that two firms could, quite legally, decide to put in a joint bid, or to agree that one bids and the other is offered a deal giving it access to the bidder's network (a 'virtual' network). If they do this, the auction might end at a lower price, which would mean that the price did not reflect the bidder's valuation, and that the government received less revenue. Collusion was a particular problem given the ownership structure of the European telecommunications industry, and rules were needed to prevent it. For example, at the time of the bid, British Telecommunications (BT) and Securicor jointly owned Cellnet: this meant that only one of the three companies was allowed to bid. Further problems were raised when, shortly before the auction, one incumbent (Vodafone) made a takeover bid for the company owning another incumbent (Orange). In this case, two bids were allowed on condition that Vodafone divested Orange immediately after the takeover, ensuring that the two licenses were in different hands.

When the government decided that it was feasible to allocate five licenses, the decision was made to go for an English auction. The five licenses were not all the same, hence bidders had to say which one they were bidding for. The main rules were as follows.

1. In each round, bids were made simultaneously, with each bidder allowed to bid only for one of the five licenses.
2. Any bidder who ceased to be 'active' (either because they held the top bid for one of the licenses or by making a new bid for a different one) had to withdraw from the auction and could not re-enter.
3. In each round, bidders who held the top bid could not change their bids or bid for different licenses. The lower bidders were allowed to put in a new bid for any of the licenses.
4. The process continued until only five bidders remained. These five had to pay the full price of the license within ten days.

An important aspect of the bidding was that, because bidders did not know what other bidders would do, there was always the possibility (even in the low early stages) that each round would be the final one. Therefore, the optimal strategy for each firm was to bid for the license where the difference between its valuation (what it thought the license was worth) and the previous bid (plus 5 per cent) was greatest.

The auction attracted thirteen bidders and went through 150 rounds over a period of eight weeks. The five final bidders included the four incumbents plus Hutchison-Whampoa, a new entrant to the UK market. One license was sold for £6 billion, three for around £4 billion, and one for £4.4 billion for a total of £22.5 billion. Not only was this much greater than had been predicted (media estimates were in the range £2–5 billion), but the government's initial view about the relative values of the different licenses proved to be wrong. The auction appears to have been successful. It clearly was successful in raising revenue and, given that the sums paid were so high, it is plausible that the licenses went to those companies that valued them most highly. Those involved in organizing the auction concluded that efficiency had been achieved. Given that five licenses were sold to separate companies, with appropriate strings attached (such as allowing users of the new network roaming access to two of the others) they also concluded that it met the second objective: ensuring competition.

Spectrum auctions in other countries were not all as successful. The UK auction raised 650 Euros per head of the population. In contrast, Switzerland raised only 20 Euros. The Swiss failed to ensure sufficient entry for bids to encourage bidders to go above the very low reserve price that had been set. When this became known, the bidders' share prices immediately rose, showing that they were getting bargains. In some countries there were legal challenges, suggesting that licenses had not gone to the company that valued them most highly. Germany raised close to the British revenue, 615 Euros per capita, but as in Austria, where only 100 Euros per capita was raised, collusion (that would have lowered the price) was strongly suspected.

The auction was undoubtedly successful in raising revenue. Whether it met the other objectives (efficiency and ensuring competition) is much less clear. The winners found themselves with large debt problems: these may not have been due entirely to the sums paid for the 3G rights but the cost of the licenses certainly contributed to the problem. As a result of its debts, BT was effectively broken up, being forced to sell Yellow Pages and to float Cellnet, which became O2. Vodafone was in serious trouble because of the enormous sums it paid for 3G licences across Europe (over 20 billion Euros). Several companies filed applications to postpone setting up 3G equipment beyond the dates specified in their contracts, raising doubts about whether new networks would be set up as quickly as had been hoped. One of the criteria for judging efficiency had been the early provision of 3G networks by firms that were organized to provide services to customers at minimum cost, and it is far from clear that this was achieved.

Where could the theory behind using an auction have been mistaken? One answer is that judgements were based on the values companies attached to licenses at a particular date. Arguments for efficiency are based on the assumption that these values reflect the best available estimates, given the information then available. However, firms may have felt under pressure to get licenses even if they had to pay sums that exceeded the expected revenues. Had an incumbent failed to bid for a license, it would have been read as indicating that it was not going to remain a major player in the mobile telecommunications industry, with effects on its share price that senior managers would have been unwilling to accept. Furthermore, the argument that the price paid for licenses constitutes a fixed cost that the firm has to pay even if it sells nothing, which will not affect price and output decisions, does not apply when there is a possibility of bankruptcy, as was certainly the case here. Debts, combined with pressures on share prices, clearly influenced company decisions in ways that may or may not be conducive to efficiency in the long term.

The way the British auction was conducted showed very clearly some of the strengths and weaknesses of economic theory. The procedures have thus been described in some detail to show that the problem was far from trivial. It involved knowledge of industrial economics in that it was necessary to analyse entry and potential collusion between firms and to design the licenses so that effective competition would be possible once the networks were built. It involved auction theory to decide how the auction should best be constructed, and theoretical predictions were tested using experimental methods. This was particularly important for two reasons. It served as a check on the theoretical results and it was more persuasive to politicians. Economics, therefore, played a major role. The outcome showed that when the objective was tightly specified (maximize revenue subject to keeping at least four firms in the industry and sell the licenses to those firms prepared to pay most for them), economic theory was extremely successful. These objectives were clearly achieved.

But this episode also shows where and why economic theory fails. If firms were the pure profit maximizers of economic theory holds them to be, if stock markets ensured that managers took a long-term view of their revenue streams, and if possible bankruptcy were not an issue, achieving the immediate objective of selling licenses to the firms prepared to pay the most for them would have ensured efficiency. However, to the extent that markets exhibit 'short-termism' and that managers are forced to pay attention to their current share price, this link breaks down. It may be that the restructuring of the telecommunications industry that followed the 3G auctions was purely a response to new information about the value of 3G licenses (the technology is always evolving, and information about demand changes all the time). However, it is equally possible that the situation reflects decisions that managers effectively were forced to take. There is a sense in which firms have only themselves to blame (they were under no legal requirement to bid), but there is also a sense in which it would have been unreasonable to expect them to do anything other than what they did. They had to try to remain in the mobile telecommunications business at any cost, and the government could therefore extract payments greater than these companies could afford. To avoid bankruptcy, firms then had to reorganize in ways that were unanticipated, the effects of which on efficiency are unknown.

MARKETS AND SOCIETY

Spectrum auctions and markets for emissions are both, despite their size and importance, small in relation to the societies in which they have been created. In both cases, market participants were firms whose managers had learned the new rules about how to work within the new markets and whose activities could be closely monitored. In this context, economic expertise proved important in designing systems that could accommodate competing pressures and, in the case of sulphur dioxide emissions, could cause efficient responses to unexpected developments.

The significance of this point is shown by contrasting the case of U.S. sulphur dioxide emissions with measures to create a market in carbon emissions to control global climate change. Though controlling sulphur dioxide emissions has implications for other countries, it was sufficient for the United States to focus on consequences that were internal at least to North America, if not the United States. Trying to control CO_2 emissions, on the other hand, has worldwide implications that matter. These are greatly exacerbated by the extremely unequal way in which both emissions and their immediate consequences are distributed across the globe. China may be one of the largest emitters of CO_2, but the United States and Europe still have much higher per capita emissions and are among the regions least likely to be affected by the consequences of climate change. More significantly, control of CO_2 emissions involves far more than controlling the way electricity is generated. Thus, where SO_2 emission control was concerned with generating the required quantity of electricity in a different way, CO_2 emission control necessitates questioning, at least in the developed countries, everyone's way of life. The economic problem and the social one cannot be separated. Thus although markets for carbon have been created, they cover only a small proportion of the world's emissions.

3

Creating a Market Economy

On 21 December 1991, a meeting of representatives of the eleven republics of the Soviet Union took the decision to dissolve the union at the end of the year, replacing it with the much looser Commonwealth of Independent States (CIS). Many powers that had previously rested with the Soviet Union were now devolved to the republics. By far, the largest republic was the Russian Federation. Its government, led by Boris Yeltsin, who had been elected President in July 1991, inherited a rapidly deteriorating economic situation. Unemployment was rising, and output falling rapidly. Prices (though still largely controlled by the state) were rising rapidly, and the ruble was clearly overvalued. Economic reform was essential, for the Soviet system was collapsing. The question facing the government was not whether or not to reform but how to do so.

Though Yeltsin had been elected by a large majority, the Russian political system was far from stable. Political criteria were inseparable from economic ones, not just because certain strategies were impossible, but also because economic decisions would affect politics. Other countries in Eastern Europe (such as Poland, Czechoslovakia and Hungary), which had begun the same transition two years earlier, could provide some guidance. However, the situation in those countries was in many ways different from that of Russia or the other former Soviet republics. They were smaller; their economies were different, and their political cultures, characterized by decades of hostility to Soviet domination, were also different.

There was a clear consensus that a transition towards a capitalist economy was needed. The Soviet model, even if not completely collapsed, was widely perceived as having failed. Nevertheless, it was hard to see how a centrally planned economy could operate in a more open society. There were questions, therefore, about the type of capitalism that should be adopted and the means by which the transition should be achieved. Was it to be the 'shock therapy' of a quick transition or something more gradual?

There were also technical questions. If state industries were to be privatized, how should this be accomplished? How could the government set up a system of taxation? What role should the state have in this new capitalist economy? How should monetary policy operate, especially when the state was running a large deficit, financed by increasing the money supply and causing inflation? How should foreign trade be liberalized and what should the role of foreign investment be? Once these and other questions were answered, there was the question of sequencing – in what order should the government implement these reforms, and how should they be linked to other changes, such as reforms of the legal system? These were not purely economic questions, but they were clearly questions on which economists ought to be able to offer advice, and many did so.

Many American and West European economists were attracted to studying problems relating to the Soviet transition to capitalism. Foreign aid became an important factor; much of it took the form of 'technical assistance' – Western experts coming in to offer expertise that was believed that Russia or other former socialist countries did not have. Much of this expertise came from business, notably, from what were then the 'Big Six' global accounting firms (now reduced to four), and did not involve economists (bearing in mind that precise disciplinary boundaries are hard to define). But economists were involved in many ventures. Academic units that became involved were the Harvard Institute for International Development (HIID) and the Centre for Economic Performance at the London School of Economics (LSE). The economists who became involved included not only the relatively small number of specialists in the Soviet Union, who typically spoke Russian and were familiar with the Soviet economic, legal and political systems, but also more prominent economists who had previously worked in other fields. Some had experience with stabilization programmes in Third World developing countries, although, because of differences between these countries and Russia, this experience was not always helpful. The same was true of experts in privatization or monetary control in Western countries. Many economists who became 'experts' on transition are best described as 'general' economists, who applied standard economic theories and techniques to the new problems. Their lack of familiarity with the existing system was a bone of contention with the Russians, for their visits were often short, and resources had to be put into briefing them about local conditions.

Faced with a choice of at least five teams offering different economic programmes, Yeltsin opted for one led by Yegor Gaidar. Gaidar had been working with a team of Russian economists who, since the opening up of the Soviet Union in the late 1980s, had been discussing how to undertake the transition to capitalism. The members of this team were young and convinced that the older generation was trapped in Marxist-Leninist ideology. They had good contacts in the West. Russian economists, including Gaidar and Anatoly Chubais (who would both go on to hold senior government posts, including Deputy Prime Minister), and worked closely with a group that included Jeffrey Sachs and Andrei Shleifer (from Harvard), Anders Åslund (from Stockholm) and Richard Layard (from LSE). This group became closely associated with Lawrence Summers, also from Harvard, who was chief economist at the World Bank from 1991 to 1993, and then Under Secretary and later Deputy Secretary at the U.S. Treasury Department under President Clinton, and who became Director of the National Economic Council under President Obama. This group directed much American aid to Russia.

The Gaidar-Chubais team advocated shock therapy – a rapid transition to capitalism. The team shared the view that Russia had to become a market economy as soon as possible, for only then could issues such as the role of the state (would Russia be a social democratic or liberal capitalist economy?) be addressed. The theory was that macroeconomic stabilization had to be undertaken very quickly. Drawing on ideas that have become widely accepted in macroeconomics, it was argued that 'swift and radical measures' were needed to create credibility and to break inflationary expectations (Åslund 1992a, p. 28). Price regulation needed to be abandoned because to retain it would be to keep inflationary expectations alive. To ensure competition, the liberalization of foreign trade and of monopolies should occur at the same time. Because high inflation made it difficult to raise revenues, and the tax system was in disarray, the government budget had to be balanced by cutting spending and abolishing subsidies. This would entail much suffering, but less than would a policy of gradual change.

Macroeconomic stabilization and the establishment of market prices were to be followed by fast and massive privatization, as rapidly as the necessary legislation could be passed. This required the rule of law and the establishment of firm property rights, but as soon as these were in place (ideally as part of the constitution), privatization could proceed. The main argument for such rapid privatization was that the command economy had failed: the state was incapable of managing enterprises, especially in a time of economic crisis. The Austrian economist, Ludwig von Mises was, Åslund claimed, right when, in 1920, he argued that 'socialism is the abolition of rational economy … Exchange relations between production-goods can only be established on the basis of private ownership of the means of production' (Åslund 1991, p. 18 and 1992a, p. 70). Private ownership would ensure financial discipline: it would introduce competition, and the existence of prices would lead to rational investment decisions. The restructuring of the economy therefore had to be based on market prices and private property. Analogies with leaping across a river were drawn: it had to be done in one jump. The important thing was to get to the other side, however this was achieved. There would be a cost, but once capitalism and a stable democracy were established, it was reasonable to expect growth rates of 8 per cent per year (Åslund 1991, p. 22).

A further rationale for shock therapy and rapid privatization was political. If change were not introduced quickly, existing vested interests would have the power to block reform. State involvement in economic activity created opportunities for corruption and should be avoided. There was a widespread feeling that if assets were not privatized, they would be taken, legally or illegally, by the old elite (the concept of *prikhvatizatsiya*, which means simply 'grabbing' or making state property one's own, sounding very much like 'privatization', already had wide currency). It was also argued that widespread private ownership was essential for the emergence of a pluralist democracy. In other words, democracy was simply not possible without privatization. The need to privatize quickly might mean that limited revenues would have to be raised by selling state assets. This should be accepted. To achieve sufficient concentration of ownership to render management accountable to shareholders, but without creating great inequality, shares should be distributed to mutual funds in which all citizens would have a stake. Economists, such as the Hungarian Janos Kornai, who argued that the state should look after its assets carefully until they could be sold to a new middle class at a real market price, were said to be misguided. No government could afford to implement a stabilization programme that would impose hardship for more than a brief period: voters would accept a short period of sacrifice, provided that they had confidence that it would not last long. Extreme importance was attached to the speed of privatization: '*speed and scale are far more important than, for instance, revenues from privatization*' (Åslund 1991, p. 30; emphasis in original).

The main international organizations involved with development supported this strategy. A report written jointly for the International Monetary Fund (IMF), the World Bank, the Organization of Economic Cooperation and Development (OECD) and the European Bank for Reconstruction and Development (EBRD) in 1990 outlined policies almost identical to those of the Gaidar-Chubais group. These policies included macroeconomic stabilization, price liberalization and the encouragement of competition, and structural change, including the establishment of secure property rights and extensive privatization, with subsidies to essential consumer goods to prevent widespread poverty. Whilst the report recognized that enormous political and legal changes would be required before effective privatization was possible, and that measures to ensure that assets were privatized equitably were needed, the emphasis was on the need for speed. It described as undesirable the policy Gorbachev announced as President of the USSR, which called for stabilization, liberalization and substantial structural reform to be undertaken over a period of eighteen months to two years, 'a relatively gradualist approach to the transition' (IMF/World Bank 1990, p. 12), because it laid out a process whereby liberalization would take place whilst a large proportion of output was, at least initially, produced by the state. The report's creators believed that this had the potential to retard restructuring with the result that liberalization might not in practice be undertaken. They concluded: 'Ideally, a path of gradual reform could be laid out which would minimize economic disturbance and lead to an early harvesting of the fruits of increased economic efficiency. But we know of no such path' (IMF/World Bank 1990, p. 2).

THE CONSEQUENCES

A policy of shock therapy was introduced at the beginning of 1992, and it had dramatic results. Industrial production and national income fell rapidly for several years. By 1998 industrial production had fallen to 45 per cent of its 1989 peak, and gross domestic product (GDP) to 55 per cent. The fall in output over the first three years was comparable to what happened in the United States during the Great Depression of 1929–32. In Russia, however, the recession lasted far longer – seven years. At the same time, price liberalization, which caused an immediate 245 per cent rise in prices, led to uncontrolled hyperinflation. The worst year was 1992, when producer prices rose over 3,000 per cent, and it took several years to bring inflation under control. Because prices of basic foodstuffs, energy and transport were still controlled by the state (a policy that itself caused problems) consumer prices fell less, but real wages nevertheless fell dramatically, by as much as 60 per cent. The transition was a catastrophe.

Though most Russians experienced enormous hardship during the years after 1992, some did not. The change is hard to measure reliably because access to goods under the communist regime depended as much on contacts, party membership and political influence as on income, but there seems little doubt that there was a spectacular increase in inequality. Such data as there are suggest that from 1993 to 1998, the share of national income going to the top 10 per cent of the population doubled, from 19 to 40 per cent. In contrast, the share going to the poorest 10 per cent more than halved. To put it differently, in 1988, the richest tenth of the population received 4.6 times as much as the poorest tenth; only five years later, they received twenty-five times as much. As a class of very rich people emerged, the proportion of Russians living in poverty rose from 2 per cent to 50 per cent. The poor went hungry, but Moscow's streets were congested with Mercedes cars.

Everyone had accepted that the transition would involve some loss of output, but no one, not even the critics of shock therapy, believed that it would be quite this bad – that the recession would last so long or would have such a disastrous effect on output and income distribution. The policy's supporters claimed that the problem was that liberalization was not undertaken fast enough. A major problem was the fixing of energy prices. Though this was designed to ease the transition, it resulted in a massive gap between Russian and world energy prices that, with trade liberalization, could be exploited: traders could buy cheap energy in Russia and export it, making an enormous profit. Had *all* prices been liberalized at once, supporters claimed, this could not have happened. Another problem was that, although the aim of liberalization was to create competition, many businesses were able to use the state bureaucracy to sustain monopolies. Corruption was rife and people continued using and exploiting the state bureaucracy as they had learned to do under the Soviet regime. Trade might now be legal, but local governments could require licenses, creating openings for bribery. Advocates of a quick transition blamed politicians, such as Victor Chernomyrdin, who replaced Gaidar as Deputy Prime Minister before being himself replaced, and members of the Duma, the Russian parliament, who had questioned the reforms. Questioning the speed of the reforms was sometimes attributed to a desire to defend vested interests.

Arguably, the biggest disaster was the way in which privatization was managed. It had been undertaken before institutions were established to enforce competition and ensure that firms met their contractual obligations. Laws and regulations to restrain monopoly were weak. The state bureaucracy could be used by businessmen to frustrate competition through either imposing regulations or relaxing them (often in exchange for bribes). The legal system was undeveloped, and because of the corruption and patronage inherited from the Soviet system, there was no law enforcement mechanism that was independent of the interested parties. In addition, some privatization was ad hoc. Managers might end up with de facto control of enterprises. There were great incentives, given the high degree of uncertainty, to engage in asset stripping rather than attempt to earn profits through productive activity, for wealth generated by asset stripping could then be moved outside the country. Successful privatization, based on broad share ownership, required a middle class that could own shares outright or in holding companies. Some people had large savings, but hyperinflation wiped these out. Finally, though considerable efforts were made to ensure that privatization took place in a reasonably equitable manner, large sections of Russian industry were privatized in a way that seemed, to many observers, designed to create a small group of immensely wealthy oligarchs who were prepared to support the government. The government borrowed money from private banks, giving shares in some of the largest and most valuable government enterprises as collateral, and then defaulted on its loans. The enterprises passed into the hands of the banks' owners for next for nothing, creating a small number of billionaires who were well placed to remove their funds to safer investments in the West.

One defence of the Russian catastrophe was that it was inevitable, given the magnitude of the changes that had to be made. The problem with this argument is that other countries, especially outside the CIS, handled the transition much better. Poland, Hungary and Czechoslovakia also experienced sharp declines in output, but they were short-lived compared with what happend in Russia, and these countries avoided many of the mistakes that were made in Russia. China pursued a gradualist policy that resulted in rapid growth, to the point where China's per capita income, which had previously been a lot lower, approached the Russian level. If the catastrophe was inevitable, it was only because of circumstances unique to Russia (or Russia along with some other states in the CIS).

But ignorance of the changes required is not the most convincing explanation of the disaster. Gaidar and Chubais were, after all, Russians who were thoroughly familiar with the way the Soviet system worked. Rather, it was a failure to understand the linkages among the various problems faced, and hence the scale of the impediments to reform. The advocates of shock therapy undoubtedly identified many of the crucial problems when, for example, they spoke of the need for a functioning legal system, effective accounting standards, managerial accountability, competition, hard budget constraints, and so on. They recognized that corruption was a major problem. However, they proceeded with macro-economic reforms and privatization even though the structural reforms necessary for them to work were not in place. These structural reforms required both 'top-down' changes and 'bottom-up' changes. Top-down changes were comparatively easy to implement. There might be political obstacles, but legislation could be passed and central government policy could be changed. Bottom-up changes were both more important and more difficult to effect. For example, firms had to learn to earn profits by selling more goods and reducing costs, not (as in the Soviet system) by manipulating the bureaucracy, breaking the rules and finding ways around the system. Trust had to be established, so that firms would supply goods without requiring payment in advance. In an environment where bending or breaking rules was norm, establishing a legal system that would enforce the payment of debts was an enormous challenge. The reformers implemented top-down changes in the belief or hope that they would induce the necessary bottom-up changes. When faced with banks that would not supply unlimited credit, firms would start to operate in a capitalist way. But this did not happen because there were still enormous opportunities for manipulating the system and people who were skilled at doing so. Firms turned to state institutions to impose regulations that preserved their monopoly powers. Individuals negotiated advantageous deals with the state and used every possible opportunity to get their money out of the country. Top-down reform did not generate bottom-up change. A remark made by Chubais, referring to the 1995 loans-for-shares deal, illustrates both the scale of the problem and the belief that, by placing resources in private hands, it would create an efficient capitalist economy:

They steal and steal and steal. They are stealing absolutely everything and it is impossible to stop them. But let them steal and take their property. They will then become owners and decent administrators of this property (Freeland 2000, p. 70).

Aside from creating a group of very wealthy people, Chubais's argument that people would become 'owners and decent administrators' of property they had stolen failed to allow for the fact that wealth was not

staying in Russia where it would be managed efficiently by its new owners. Instead, it was immediately moved abroad, in the massive flight of
capital out of Russia that characterized the transition process. In short,
there was no short cut: the interactions of various reforms meant that
transition was a far more complicated process than anyone appreciated
at the time.

THE ROLE OF ECONOMISTS

To what extent is it possible to argue that what happened in Russia was a
failure of economics? Even if the catastrophe had been avoidable, can the
blame not simply be placed on those who managed the process, including successive Russian governments (and their Soviet predecessors) and
their advisers? It is certainly true that the crucial decisions were made
by Russian politicians, and even when individuals made honest attempts
to take decisions that were in the national interest, the political environment created enormous problems. The speed at which decisions had to
be made did not allow for extensive discussion, and the government had
limited control over what was happening. However, Western economists
were involved in the process in significant ways. First, international organizations such as the IMF and the World Bank played a major role by providing financial and technical assistance. Second, the Russian reformers
were well versed in Western economics, and their advisers were eminent
Western economists. These factors were important because the Gaidar-
Chubais group's position was to a great extent legitimated by their links
to the West. Western economics was not neutral; it played an important role in the political processes inside Russia. (Conversely, the links
between western economists and the Gaidar-Chubais group were a reason why much U.S. aid was channelled through the HIID.) Had Western
economics been different, the dynamics of the Russian political process
might have led to a different outcome: there is no reason to believe that
this was likely, but it is possible.

However, even if economists are implicated, there remains the question of whether it is possible to use the episode to draw conclusions
about economics in general. It could be argued that the bad outcome

amounted to no more than an indictment of the individuals and organizations involved. Some economists had warned that markets did not
always operate in the textbook manner, and others had expressed doubts
about IMF structural adjustment policies and stabilization programs in
other countries. It is arguable that the reformers chose to take certain
ideas from economics and to ignore others, which would make it ridicu-
lous to blame economics in general. It might be different if there were
unanimity amongst economists, but there is not. The transition away
from Communism followed very different paths in other countries of the
former Soviet bloc: Hungary, Poland and the Czech Republic, as noted,
were all very different. This is undoubtedly a very powerful argument but
against it lies the fact that the thinking that underlay the management of
the Russian transition echoes themes that are pervasive in contemporary
economics.

The basic premise underlying shock therapy was that socialism could
not work and that capitalism, however shaky the institutional foundations, would be preferable. Economic theory has contributed to this view
in several ways. First, economics is dominated by the theory of supply
and demand in perfectly competitive markets. According to this theory,
prices will adjust so as to make the demand for every good equal to
the amount that suppliers want to sell, and the resulting allocation of
resources will be efficient in the sense that any departure from it would
make at least one person worse off. Economists have long been aware of
conditions under which this theory will not work – reasons for 'market
failure': competition may be imperfect, buyers and sellers may not be
fully informed, or the cost to individuals of an activity may not be the
same as its cost to society (for example, the producer may not have to
bear the cost of pollution).

However, whilst virtually all economists are well aware of these reasons for market failure, in practice, they often ignore them or treat them
as being of secondary importance. The theory of supply and demand is
intuitively appealing to many economists and has a simplicity that makes
it easy to explain to non-economists. Thus, although Russian policy
makers were responsible for the catastrophe, their policies flowed naturally from prejudices and presuppositions that have come to dominate

economics. As Joseph Stiglitz puts it, referring to the choice between socialism and capitalism:

[T]he competitive paradigm not only did not provide much guidance on the vital question of the choice of economic systems but what 'advice' it did provide was often misguided. The conceptions of the market that underlay that analysis mischaracterized it; the standard analyses underestimated the strengths – and weaknesses – of market economies and accordingly provided wrong signals for the potential success of alternatives and for how the market might be improved upon. By the same token, that paradigm cannot be relied upon to provide guidance to the former socialist economies as they seek to build new economic systems. (Stiglitz 1994, p. 5)

However, the problem was not simply that economists paid insufficient attention to market structures and departures from the standard theory of perfect competition; it was that they failed to pay enough attention to the institutions of capitalism, that is, to the institutions that make market economies work. Journalists and political scientists may talk about 'Anglo-Saxon' versus 'German', 'French' or 'Japanese' forms of capitalism, but such terminology is absent from most academic work and from most curricula. Even the word 'capitalism' is used rarely: economists are much more likely to talk about markets. Here, the distinction between markets with one seller (monopolies), a small number of sellers (oligopolies) or many (competitive markets) is useful, but it is a thin framework for analysing capitalist institutions.

It can also be argued that economists pay comparatively little attention to the adverse effects of an unequal income distribution. The positive effects are easy to explain and to model using standard theory: larger prizes will make people work harder to get them. But the negative effects of inequality, such as the way it can undermine social cohesion or increase the barriers to social mobility, are rarely considered. Because the negative effects are hard to analyse within an individualistic framework, such analysis is typically left to sociologists. Further, few economists attach much importance to the issue of who owns property. Economists generally presume, in line with Chubais's remark, quoted on page 45 above, that if property is privately owned it will be looked after well. In addition the so-called Coase theorem, which states (very loosely) that if there are no transaction costs (costs attached to the process of negotiating, implementing and enforcing contracts), the allocation of resources will be the same regardless of who owns property rights, is used to justify ignoring the distribution of property rights. Ownership will affect the distribution of income, but it should not affect the efficiency with which resources are used. Of course, this conclusion does not hold if there are transaction costs, but the neglect of transaction costs is a consequence of paying too little attention to the institutions of capitalism.

Finally, economists pay insufficient attention to the distribution of income and wealth across individuals because the most widely used welfare criterion is Pareto efficiency. A Pareto efficient allocation of resources is one where it is impossible to make anyone better off without at the same time making someone else worse off. It is attractive to economists because it makes it possible to draw conclusions about social welfare without making the ethical judgements that are necessary if one is to compare one person's well being with that of another. There is, according to the dominant view, no scientific basis for saying that taking £1,000 from John and giving it to Rachel will raise or lower welfare even if John is already much wealthier than Rachel. The result is that questions of distribution, which are by definition about one person having less and another having more, are ignored as being beyond the scope of economic science.

There is, therefore, a sense in which economists are justified in claiming innocence. Theories of market failure do exist, and they can be used to explain many of the things that went wrong in Russia. However, perhaps because markets appear to work smoothly most of the time in developed economies, economists tend to treat problems like those that were crucial in Russia, such as the lack of institutions that support competitive markets, transaction costs, divergences between private and social costs, the unequal ownership of resources and the distribution of income, as secondary concerns. Emphasizing, as many introductory economics textbooks do, the near-miraculous power of the market, rather than the problems made it much easier for the Russian reformers to claim legitimacy for disastrous policies.

The case of the Russian transition to capitalism highlights the failure of economists to pay sufficient attention to institutions. There are economists who focus on institutions (note the award of the 2009 Nobel Memorial Prize in Economic Science to Oliver Williamson for his work on the firm and Elinor Ostrom for her work on communally owned resources) but much of the time economics either ignores them or focuses on a limited range of institutions. Institutional design has become a major area of economics, but the attention is on the design of individual markets, not the operation of economic systems as a whole. Economists generally talk about market economies rather than capitalist ones, deflecting attention from the fact that the institutions of capitalism are not homogeneous. The result is that whilst economists have had successes in designing institutions on a small scale, as in the U.S. market for SO_2 emissions, designing auctions, they can provide much less useful guidance when dealing with problems that involve entire societies, the operation of which depends on a complex web of social and economic institutions. It may well be the case that there was neither the time to design institutions that would have made it possible to have less catastrophic transition to capitalism nor the political power to put them into place, but it did not help that economics was dominated by abstract theories that paid scant attention to the institutions needed for capitalism to function properly.

Globalization and Welfare

Globalization is a very broad phenomenon, that cannot be discussed comprehensively in a short chapter. However, it raises important issues about modern economics. It concerns a doctrine – free trade – for which there is very wide support indeed among economists. Yet, quite apart from the anti-globalization movement associated with, for example Naomi Klein's *No Logo* (2000), there are economists who question whether the gains resulting from globalization may outweigh the harm that they see it doing. Even if they support the idea of globalization, they find much to criticize about the way it is happening. Globalization is thus an issue that forces attention on ideology – on certain beliefs that are deeply held by many economists and that appear to critics to be prejudices – and on why conflicting opinions are so difficult to resolve that it can seem to outsiders that economists cannot agree on anything.

To reach conclusions about whether globalization is good or bad, it is necessary to answer two question 'What are the consequences of globalisation?' and 'Do these consequences raise or lower social welfare?' Answering the first question means considering issues such as whether trade liberalization raises a country's income or whether the free movement of labour and capital raises incomes for the poor. These involve 'positive' economics and relate to things that economists should, in principle, be able to resolve using scientific methods. Answering the second question requires making ethical judgements about what constitutes social welfare, and hence about how the changes produced by

globalization contribute to it. Because this is a 'normative' question –
about how things ought to be – it cannot be answered without making
ethical judgements about what is good or bad. Globalization is thus an
area in which there is enormous potential for economists' conclusions
to be influenced by their political ideologies or their ethical judgements
about what makes for a good society.

Globalization is closely linked to the problem of economic development: Why is it that some countries have become rich whilst others
remain poor? Though some economists have offered simple diagnoses
and remedies, this is widely agreed to be a complex problem involving factors as diverse as political stability, education, investment, and
the existence of a commercial culture, many of which extend beyond
the remit of economics. Lack of consensus about the factors that affect
economic development is another reason why economists disagree over
globalization.

THE WORLD ECONOMY AFTER 1945

Globalization is about the economies of the world becoming more open
to each other and as a result more integrated. It involves the reduction of
tariff barriers and regulations that inhibit trade and make it difficult for
capital and labour to move from one country to another. In a perfectly
globalized world, people are able to move and work wherever they like
and invest as freely in other countries as in their own; and firms can sell
their products internationally and source their raw materials from any-
where in the world. Globalization, therefore, requires an international
monetary system so that payments can take place; a system of international law that makes it possible for parties in one country to enter
into and enforce contracts with parties in other countries; adequate protection of property rights, and a harmonization of regulations so that
products do not have to go through a complex approval process in every
country in which they are sold.

The European Union provides a clear illustration. It began as a regional
association based on a commitment by six countries (Belgium, France,
Germany, Italy, Luxemburg and the Netherlands) to integrate a limited
number of markets, starting with coal and steel, and developed into a

customs union in which goods could flow freely between member countries. However, it was recognized that to create a true single market, it was necessary to go further: there had to be common standards for products, educational qualifications had to be recognized from one country to another, and so on. Such measures came about much more slowly than the removal of tariff barriers.

The recent movement towards globalization started at the end of the Second World War. After the virtual collapse of international trade during the 1930s when, in response to the Great Depression, countries raised tariff barriers and engaged in competitive currency devaluations to protect employment. Attempts were made to create a managed world economic order: the Bretton Woods system, named after the town in New Hampshire where the agreement was signed in 1944. The Bretton Woods agreement created an international monetary system in which currencies were (at least eventually) freely convertible into U.S. dollars, and hence into gold at known exchange rates. There was also to be a movement towards freer trade and a reduction of tariff barriers. Unlike in the 1920s, international institutions were set up to ensure the smooth functioning of the system: the International Bank for Reconstruction and Development, now known as the World Bank, the IMF and the General Agreement on Tariffs and Trade, which later became the World Trade Organization (WTO).

The Bretton Woods system was an attempt to create a managed world economy, but it fell far short of globalization as the term is understood today. It did result in considerable integration and an enormous expansion of world trade, especially among developed countries, but integration was far from complete; many barriers to movement of capital, labour and goods remained. The globalization movement as it is now understood is of a more recent origin and rests on different foundations. The reasons for this are too varied to be considered here, but they include the experiences in the 1970s and 1980s, when the post-war international monetary system broke down and the World Bank and IMF came to play a very different role, focusing less on the developed economies of Western Europe, North America, Japan and Australasia and more on the Third World – Latin America, Asia and Africa. The fixed exchange-rate system, that had lasted since 1944, collapsed in 1971. The

1970s were a decade of worldwide high inflation which caused attitudes
about managing economies to change dramatically, as could be seen in
the policies of Margaret Thatcher in the United Kingdom and Ronald
Reagan in the United States.

When oil prices rose sharply following the Iranian revolution in 1979,
governments in the United States and Europe raised interest rates to prevent inflation from rising as far as it had risen after the oil-price rises
of 1973–4. The result was a debt crisis in many Third World countries.
These countries had taken on large debts during the 1970s and were suddenly faced with dramatic rises in the interest payments on these debts.
Because the developed countries were experiencing recession, Third
World countries could not raise the funds by increasing exports, and so
were faced with prospect of not being able to meet their obligations. The
IMF and the World Bank became much more heavily involved in their
economic and financial affairs. In particular, these organizations began
to help design and implement internal reforms in Third World countries because it was believed that without such reforms there was little
prospect that countries in the Third World would be able to achieve the
necessary payments on their loans (or what remained of their loans after
the rescheduling negotiations).

The 'second round' of international integration came during the following decades. It was based less on a managed economy than on market
liberalization. Countries engaged in tariff reductions that were mediated
through the successive negotiating rounds of the WTO; more contro-
versially, the IMF and the World Bank sought to establish free-market
conditions, advocating policies to guarantee property rights, the privatization of public services and state-run industries, opening up of capital
markets to foreign investors, and enabling of foreign firms to compete
in countries' domestic markets. The result was the emergence of a situation where powerful institutions, dominated by the United States and
other developed countries, were seen as forcing Third World countries
to open up their economies to Western-dominated multinational firms
with which smaller domestic producers could not compete. At the same
time, although many of these policies had been followed in the developed
economies (Britain, for example, had been a pioneer of privatization),
and many countries had experienced extensive deregulation, there were

voices that claimed they represented a dual standard: Third World countries were being forced to open up their markets but Europe, Japan and the United States continued to protect agriculture, the sector in which Third World countries had greatest chance of competing effectively.

Globalization was thus seen as embodying a particular ideology, often labelled 'neo-liberal' to distinguish it from nineteenth-century liberalism. It focused on the property rights that were relevant for business rather than on, say, protecting workers' rights or establishing environmental-safety standards. It advocated competition, yet appeared indifferent to the monopoly power exerted by large international firms. It involved the opening of capital markets, enabling rich countries to gain control over poor countries' industries, whilst poor countries had no control over policies pursued in rich countries. Unlike at the United Nations (UN), where each country has one vote, irrespective of size or wealth, voting power in the IMF and the World Bank is strictly linked to economic power, meaning that the Third World has very little influence.

It is not just in the Third World where these concerns were felt. In Europe and the United States, liberalization was felt to harm the interests of workers as it often involved measures to restrict the influence of trade unions, attacks on social security systems, privatization, the contracting out of public services to the private sector, less secure employment conditions, and moves away from progressive taxation (progressive taxes are ones that result in the rich paying a higher proportion of their income in taxes than do the poor). Jobs were thought threatened, either from immigrants who were willing to accept lower wages and less secure conditions of employment than native workers (this is true *a fortiori* where workers are illegal and face the threat of deportation if they are discovered by the authorities) or through outsourcing (where companies contract operations out to suppliers in other countries), not to mention competition from goods produced abroad at costs that are believed to be low because of low wages and sub-standard working conditions that would not be allowed in Europe or the United States.

Such factors are widely believed to lie behind the dramatic rise in inequality that has taken place in many countries. In Britain, the United States, and in many other developed countries, the distribution of income had become progressively more equal until the 1970s, after which inequality began to rise. These trends reflect many factors: economic factors include changes in technology affecting demand for skilled and unskilled workers, and competition from low-income countries; political or social factors include changes in tax policies and redistribution of income through measures such as unemployment benefits, free education and health care provision. What is clear is that, taking the period from the 1970s to the 2000s as a whole, top incomes rose much more rapidly than low incomes, producing greater inequality. Some data suggest that incomes at the bottom of the distribution stagnated in real terms (that money incomes did not rise faster than prices), whilst other statistics suggest that low incomes did rise but very slowly. Either way, the picture is consistent with the notion that globalization contributed to a significant increase in inequality, although, because inequality also depends on social factors, it is hard to prove any simple cause-and-effect relationship.

It is worth concluding by noting that though people speak of globalization as something radically new, it is not the first time that the world economy has become more integrated. One might speak of long swings to and from integration over many centuries. The invention of the telegraph and steamships in the nineteenth century probably had an effect that was as great as anything that has happened in the past half century. If economic integration has happened before, is globalization really a new phenomenon? The obvious response is that, even if economic integration is far from new, it is now taking place on a scale that has no previous parallel. However, scale alone is hardly grounds for claiming that it amounts to a new phenomenon. There is also a danger in failing to recognize the pervasive social changes that integration brought about in the nineteenth century. A Victorian Englishman wanting to talk to his local bank, for example, would not have found himself talking to a call centre in Bangalore, but his consumption patterns were transformed by the empire and the expansion of world trade. Of more significance than simple scale, perhaps, is the connection between globalization and economic development. Globalization now matters because it is so closely linked to the development of the Third World. But again, the differences from earlier generations should not be exaggerated. Indians living in Victoria's empire were extremely aware of the state of their economy relative to the British economy, and they drew conclusions about how this was linked to trade and empire. What has changed is the political context that has altered the way economic development has been conceived.

There is also the question of institutions. Economic integration in the nineteenth century involved free trade, though some countries retained protective tariffs, just as today. However, firms remained based in one country, trading with firms in other countries. Today, globalization is driven by large multinational firms as much as by governments. This means that countries are linked by corporate administrative structures that go beyond markets and are substantially independent of governments. Production can be planned on a global scale in a way that was not possible before, and this international dimension of production has significant implications for national policies.

ECONOMISTS AND GLOBALIZATION

Economists have long been known as supporters of free trade. The phrase *laissez-faire, laissez-passer*, meaning 'let people do what they want and go where they like', is about three hundred years old. Some economists consider it heretical even to question the idea of free trade: to deny it is to cast doubt on one's credentials as an economist. How do economists justify this strongly held belief in free trade? One argument is that increasing the size of the market increases scope for the division of labour (for specialization, either within the firm or between firms), and hence for cost reduction. However, the main support for the idea of free trade is the doctrine of comparative advantage. Loosely, the doctrine of comparative advantage states that global production will be maximized if every country specializes in the goods it is best at producing compared with other countries. Thus, it may be that Japan can manufacture both aircraft and cars more cheaply than Europe, but if the productivity gap is greater in cars than in aircraft, it may be better for Japan to export cars to Europe and use the proceeds to buy aircraft rather than producing aircraft itself. If Europe has lower productivity in all industries, its workers will be paid less, enabling its goods to compete in countries where productivity is higher. Tariffs and other barriers to free trade are harmful because they distort production away from the pattern dictated by comparative advantage.

The theory of comparative advantage ties in with a related idea, that if there is perfect competition – a state in which firms have no market power because if they were to raise prices above their market levels, other firms would immediately take away their business – production will be organized as efficiently as it can be. Taxes, subsidies, monopolies and other barriers to competition are harmful because they distort production. Like the doctrine of comparative advantage, this idea can be formulated very precisely and the results rigorously demonstrated. Thus we know, with certainty, that if markets are perfectly competitive and certain other assumptions are satisfied, the resulting equilibrium will be one in which it would be impossible to make anyone better off without making someone else worse off – it is 'Pareto efficient'. This theorem and one closely related to it are commonly known as the two fundamental theorems of welfare economics. Economists generally do not believe markets are perfectly competitive (casual observation is enough to establish that many markets are oligopolistic and that firms engage in advertising and other activities that one would not find in perfectly competitive markets), but it is generally assumed that they are sufficiently competitive that the theory will give useful results. Competition will force firms to use the most efficient technologies, and high profits will not last indefinitely as other firms compete for their business.

The measures that are either advocated or criticized as part of globalization are often called 'the Washington consensus', a term coined by John Williamson in 1990 to describe the measures being urged on Latin American countries by various agencies in Washington, notably the IMF and the World Bank. These include factors such as fiscal discipline, lowering marginal tax rates, trade liberalization, removal of barriers to foreign investment, privatization of state industry, deregulation, and the establishment of secure property rights. This is a package of measures aimed at creating conditions in which markets can work and competitive activity is encouraged. In a dynamic context, competition does not mean that firms cannot make profits by raising their prices and restricting their output: it means that they are induced to produce new products that consumers want and that they find ways to reduce costs through innovation. Free markets and the package of measures involved in the Washington consensus are believed likely to make it attractive for foreign and multinational firms to invest, introducing new products and stimulating domestic producers to innovate.

However, while it is possible to find good reasons in support of all these arguments, they cannot be proved to be correct. There are models, for example, of, innovation in specific markets, but a genuinely dynamic system involving an entire society undergoing technical change is too complicated to formally model. It even becomes difficult to model how markets work in a dynamic world where firms have some monopoly power and competition takes the form of new firms and innovation. Theoretical models may suggest processes that should be at work, but it is hard to prove what is going on through deduction alone.

One type of evidence comes from looking at detailed case studies of development policy since the Second World War. William Easterly has provided a catalogue of what he describes as 'panaceas that failed': using foreign aid to raise investment in developing countries; raising the level of education; giving away contraceptives to reduce unwanted births; lending to poor countries that had not learned to control inflation. In all of these cases, policies were based on then-fashionable ideas about how to promote development. In contrast, the successes of development are centred on the idea that 'People respond to incentives'. Easterly summarizes the basic principle of economics in two ways: 'People do what they get paid to do; what they don't get paid to do, they don't do'; 'People respond to incentives; all the rest is commentary' (Easterley 2002, p. xii). He translates it into development economics in the following way,

If we do the hard work of ensuring that the trinity of First World aid donors, Third World governments, and ordinary Third World citizens have the right incentives, development will happen. If they don't, it won't.

The failures of development economics, Easterley argues, arose from policies that violated these basic economic principles.

Evidence also comes from larger studies of countries that did or did not succeed. It is commonly claimed that the collapse of the Soviet system shows that central planning cannot work and that free markets are clearly superior. More careful studies focus on countries that are comparable yet whose economic performance has been very different. Williamson has written,

> There is a lot of evidence – although not all of it is rigorous enough to satisfy the profession's econometric purists – that competitive markets and an open trade policy are in fact good for welfare. … The most compelling evidence of the virtues of competitive markets over central planning is the superior long-term performance of market over planned systems that started off at similar levels: compare Austria with Czechoslovakia, East with West Germany, Estonia with Finland, mainland China with Taiwan, North with South Korea. (Williamson 1994, p. 16)

This is where disagreements begin. For it can be argued that there are complications with many of these examples. East and West Germany were in a comparable position at the end of the Second World War, yet the East was stripped of capital by the Soviet Union. Similar factors applied in Czechoslovakia, although not to the same extent. Furthermore, Soviet planning took account not simply of economic objectives but also political ones: it was important that the countries of Eastern Europe remain within its bloc, and economic means were part of the process whereby these objectives were achieved. Comparing mainland China, an enormous rural economy receiving little outside support, with a small island, Taiwan, in which the United States had a clear strategic interest, is obviously problematic. It can also be argued that countries such as South Korea or Taiwan, though non-Communist, were following policies that were a far cry from free-market liberalism. They were certainly open economies with private enterprise, but investment was planned by industrial conglomerates with active government support and considerable protection. These objections to what Williamson describes as 'the most compelling evidence' certainly do not establish either that centrally planned economies are superior or that market economies cannot work, but they do suggest that such evidence needs to be weighed carefully.

The argument that protection may be able to promote growth has long been familiar to economists as the 'infant industry' argument recognized in the mid-nineteenth century by John Stuart Mill. Even if a country's industry is not competitive, protection may be able to nurture it to the point where it can support itself, and then the protection can be removed. It can be argued that most developed countries achieved their current position through protective trade policy: Germany and the United States in the late nineteenth century and Japan in the twentieth are the most obvious examples. And the experiences in these countries can be made into a general historical argument that it is only when countries reach a certain stage of development that they can afford free trade. If this is correct, it means that the free-market policies currently being promoted with the aid of the IMF and the World Bank are ensuring that Third World countries will be unable to develop, that is, unable to develop their industries to stand on their own against foreign competition.

Though the infant industry argument refers to international trade, similar arguments can be made more generally. Governments may need to step in either where the private sector cannot do something or where the private sector could in principle do something but in practice does not. Joseph Stiglitz gives an example of a chicken-rearing industry that was started with support from outside, and a government guarantee to buy and market the chickens once they had been reared. The government was told that such activity should be left to the private sector and withdrew, causing the industry to fail: small farmers were not willing to take the risk of buying newly-hatched chicks without knowing whether they could sell them when they had been reared. A private marketing organization *could* have emerged but did not do so in time for the industry to survive. This is an example of a 'sequencing' problem, relating to the order in which activities are liberalized. In this case, it was crucial that marketing be established before small producers became involved in production. (Exactly the same type of problem arose in the Russian transition, discussed in Chapter 3) Other sequencing questions include whether capital markets should be liberalized before or after goods markets. The costs of getting it wrong make a case for government intervention.

Such arguments hinge on the government's role in the economy. For the argument against free markets is that government can do better: it can create an environment where industries with high potential are encouraged but those without such potential are not, and where such high-potential industries are encouraged to innovate rather than merely enjoy the profits that arise from protection and high prices. India (prior to its economic reforms in the 1990s) and the Soviet Union can be cited as counters to the successes of Japan and South Korea. In both countries, central planning and bureaucracy arguably stifled initiative and diverted investment into unprofitable 'prestige' projects. India, for example, should probably never have tried to develop the large steel industry that featured high in its Five-Year plans.

The argument against state intervention is, however, not simply or even primarily inductive. If everyone is concerned with his or her own welfare, and if this depends on his or her own income, then everyone, including government officials and politicians, will be focusing on their own income, not on the general 'public interest'. The application of this idea to the public sector has come to be known as 'public choice' theory, and it is best illustrated with an example. One of the problems associated with government regulation is that if the state has the power to impose protective tariffs or impose regulations, it may be more profitable for firms to invest resources in lobbying for favourable treatment than to invest in productive activities. Not only will resources be diverted into such 'unproductive' activities but politicians will have an incentive to respond to such pressures. Government decisions will therefore not reflect the interests of society at large (however they are defined) but rather the interests of those in a position to influence the political process. Democratic processes might mitigate this behaviour, but they are likely to be too weak to control it. These problems will be particularly great in many Third World countries where governance structures are weak. It is easy for supporters of free markets and liberalization to point to instances where resources have been diverted into the pockets of individuals rather than being used to serve a broader interest.

GLOBALIZATION, INEQUALITY AND POVERTY

Economists, in general, readily conclude that globalization is desirable, often responding very strongly indeed to suggestions that restrictions on trade or capital movement might be beneficial. But beneficial to whom? No one doubts that some people benefit; the question is whether this is at the expense of others who are less able to take advantage of the opportunities offered or whose traditional livelihoods are destroyed by competition. Globalization has been defended for lifting people out of poverty and for reducing the inequality in the world; it has been criticized for failing to solve the problem of poverty and for increasingly creating societies in which the distribution of wealth is even more unequal. This raises the question of why it is so difficult to settle what appears to be a simple factual dispute.

One of the most widely used measures of poverty is the number of people living on less than U.S. $1 a day. It was used by the President of the World Bank, James Wolfensohn, to argue that in the 1980s and 1990s (the era of liberalization) the number of people living in absolute poverty fell for the first time in centuries: 'Over the past 20 years the number of people living on less than $1 a day has fallen by 200 million, after rising steadily for 200 years' (quoted in Wade 2004, p. 571). This statement seems simple enough, but even such apparently simple statistics are fraught with problems. First, the surveys on which much of the evidence rests are prone to significant errors because people do not remember correctly and because publicly provided benefits, which do not have to be paid for, may not be included. Second, local currencies have to be converted to U.S. dollar equivalents. The usual method is to use what are known as 'purchasing power parity' (PPP) exchange rates, which are based on the cost of goods in different countries. There are conceptual problems with PPP (having to do with deciding what goods to include and which prices to use in markets where goods do not all sell at the same prices). In addition, some countries did not participate in the studies that form the basis of PPP numbers. Third, because of the way incomes are distributed, the poverty numbers are highly sensitive to the choice of poverty line: choosing $1.10 or $0.90 instead of $1 can make an enormous difference to the results. These are just three of many technical problems involved in a simple index of poverty. The point of listing them is not to say that poverty cannot be measured or to claim that official statistics should not be believed (though it has been argued that there are good reasons to be very sceptical about them). It is merely to make it clear that the poverty measurement is more difficult than might appear.

An alternative way to measure poverty is to adopt a relative measure. The criterion of $1 a day, where the dollar is adjusted for differences in the cost of living across countries and for changes in the cost of living over time, is an attempt to measure poverty in an absolute sense. In theory, someone on the poverty line (getting exactly $1 a day) should be able to buy exactly the same goods wherever they are and at whatever time they are living. The strictest possible definition of poverty would be an income that allows a diet just sufficient to avoid starvation and the bare minimum of other essentials to avoid death from, say, cold. Or it could be set higher than this, as an income that allows people to live reasonably healthy lives. This is still an absolute definition, fixed in relation to biological needs.

However, it can be argued that a more meaningful definition of poverty is that one's income is too low to enable full participation in society. This might, for example, mean an income high enough that one's children can go to school, or it might be more broadly defined. But when poverty is defined in this way it moves towards a relative definition of poverty. To participate in normal social activities in the United States or Western Europe requires a higher income than it requires in, say, an Indian or African village. In Western Europe it would be reasonable to consider households that are without electricity or unable to afford a television as poor, even though such things would be considered luxuries in other parts of the world. Thus, in considering poverty in Britain, there is a strong case for using not a criterion such as the minimum wage but one such as whether people earn half, or perhaps even two-thirds, of the average level of earnings. The latter means that as society becomes wealthier, the poverty line rises in proportion.

From relative poverty, it is a short step to the distribution of income and the problem of inequality. This is conceptually quite different from poverty, even if a relative measure of poverty is used. It is possible for income to become more unequally distributed without affecting poverty at all. Suppose that average income and the income of the poor do not change at all, but there is a transfer of resources from middle–income groups, which are above the poverty line, to the very rich. Inequality will have increased but poverty does not change at all.

Some of these conceptual problems are illustrated in Table 4.1, which shows the proportion of total income received by each decile (tenth) of the population. Complete equality would mean that each decile would receive exactly one tenth of the total income, but in no country is this the case. In the United States, the bottom decile received only 1.9 per cent,

Table 4.1. *Income distribution in the 1980s*

Decile	Netherlands	Sweden	USA
1	4.2	3.3	1.9
2	6	6.2	3.8
3	6.9	7.4	5.5
4	7.9	8.4	6.8
5	8.8	9.3	8.2
6	9.7	10.2	9.5
7	10.8	11.1	11.2
8	12.1	12.3	13.3
9	13.9	13.7	16.1
10	19.7	18.1	23.7

Source: Atkinson 1995, p. 53.

whilst the top decile received almost a quarter of total income. On average members of the top decile received 12.5 times the income of people
in the bottom decile (23.7 divided by 1.9). The corresponding figure for
Sweden was 5.5, and the Netherlands was just over 4.5. Sweden and the
Netherlands appear to be much more equal societies. However, the problem with such numbers is that they look merely at the top and bottom 10
per cent of the distribution. To get a full picture, it would also be necessary to compare the top 1 per cent with the bottom 1 per cent, the top 25
per cent with the bottom 25 per cent, the top 1 per cent with the bottom
50 per cent, and so on. In general, these comparisons could all give different results. A different way of measuring inequality is needed.

Figure 4.1 shows the same data in a graph: complete equality would
mean the bottom 10 per cent would have 10 per cent of income, the bottom 20 per cent would have 20 per cent, and so on, as represented by the
straight line. The degree of inequality is shown by the distance the country is from this line. Here, the United States is clearly more unequal than
either Sweden or the Netherlands. On the other hand, compare Sweden
and the Netherlands. The curves for these two countries cross: at the
bottom of the income distribution (the bottom decile) the Netherlands is
more equal whereas higher up, Sweden is more equal. When compared
with the United States, the differences are very small, but they illustrate
the principle that it is necessary to consider the whole of the distribution,
not just one or two points on it. A measure that is commonly used for

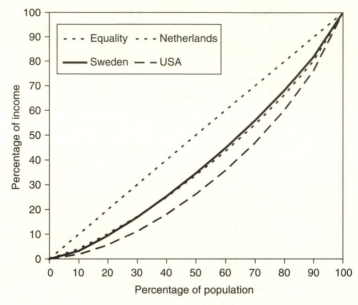

Figure 4.1: Income distribution: Netherlands, Sweden and the United States in the 1980*s*
Source: Atkinson 1995, p. 53.

this is the Gini coefficient, calculated as the size of the lens-shaped area between the equality line and the country's line in relation to the size of the triangle under the equality line. However, even this measure has limitations. For example, if we attach a very high weight to what the poorest group gets, we should consider Sweden (where the bottom decile gets only 3.3%) as more unequal than the Netherlands (where it gets 4.2%), even if the Netherlands had the higher Gini coefficient.

These seemingly technical problems in measuring inequality become very important when considering the effects of globalization. The most obvious development in the 1990s and 2000s has been a large rise in incomes at the very top of the income distribution, say, the top 1 per cent and even more so for the top 0.1 per cent (the top thousandth of the population), especially in the United States and Britain. There has also been a tendency for the bottom end of the distribution to fall behind the middle, though whether or not this is associated with a rise in poverty depends very much on how poverty is defined and is subject to great uncertainty due to the measurement problems discussed above. Thus, even a critic of the World Bank's statistics can write that 'It is plausible, and important, that the proportion of the world's population living in extreme poverty has probably fallen over the past two decades or so' even though incomes have become much more unequal (Wade 2004, p. 581). However, this conclusion is subject to great uncertainty because of measurement problems. Given rapid population growth in many poor countries, it is also possible that the absolute number of people living in extreme poverty has risen.

When considering the world as a whole there is a further issue – the relationship between households and countries. There is inequality between countries and also within countries. The former is relatively easy to calculate using average national incomes, but it does not give an accurate picture of the distribution of income across households because there are many poor people in rich countries and many wealthy people in poor countries. Furthermore, size differences between countries can cause great problems. China, which contains over a sixth of the word's population and, to a lesser extent, India pose a particular problem. Because of their size, trends in the world distribution of income across households are dominated by what happens in China and India. Much of the reduction in poverty of recent years has taken place in China. To understand why this matters, it is necessary to explore why inequality matters.

There are two main responses to arguments about the importance of inequality. The first is the argument that what matters are overall living standards, not how households' incomes compare with those of other households. The second, often coupled with the first, is that incentives are the driving force behind economic growth, and inequality creates incentives. If a factory manager earns ten times what a shop-floor worker earns, then the shop-floor worker will have a stronger incentive to work harder, acquire relevant skills or do whatever is needed to become a manager. From this perspective, inequality is not something to be worried about: indeed, it should be welcomed, so long as the poor are not actually made worse off. Poverty matters, but it can be cured by stimulating economic growth and, at least in principle, this can happen without reducing inequality. It may therefore be the case that trade liberalization, privatization, and the other measures advocated by the World Bank and the IMF create inequality but at the same time increase opportunities and incentives, thereby stimulating the growth of industry that will create work for the poor. If countries turn their back on such measures, the result will be stagnation and even greater poverty. Working long hours in an Asian sweatshop or producing agricultural products for a fraction of what they sell for in European or American markets may seem like exploitation, but the real danger is having no income at all.

Against this, it is often argued that the benefits of globalization are frequently not felt by the bulk of the poor and that the poor may even find their position made worse, not better. Skills that once enabled people to earn a living in traditional industries may become irrelevant with the advent of more modern industry. There may develop classes that simply do not fit into the 'advanced' sector of the economy or, if they can adjust to change, can do so only at high personal cost, whether in terms of lost income or a lost way of life. Perhaps more importantly, especially in the long term, local people may lose control because production may be controlled from abroad, reducing opportunities for local entrepreneurship. This is not to argue against globalization (though critics of liberalization are routinely accused of doing so); it is simply to question the way in which globalization takes place. The effects of increased openness may depend on how reforms are introduced and, to use a term mentioned earlier, the sequencing of reforms.

There are also reasons that inequality may not raise efficiency. Incentives may be important, and it may be the case that a moderate level of inequality may be useful, but it does not follow that extreme levels of inequality have the same effects. If the gap between rich and poor becomes too large, incentives may be reduced rather than increased and social mobility may also be reduced (as has happened in the United States and Britain, where children from low-income families are much less likely to become wealthy than are similar children in Scandinavia). Given that people commonly compare themselves to people with higher incomes, increased inequality may lower welfare. Studies that use questionnaires to measure well-being directly routinely show that status, which depends on someone's position relative to others, is a very important factor affecting welfare. Inequality within countries is also associated with rising crime, and inequality between countries with increased migration, both of which have significant effects on welfare.

Careful handling of evidence becomes very important. Cross-country inequality has fallen since about 1980 because the world's two most populous countries, China and India, have grown rapidly. This makes it harder to argue that liberalization has reduced inequality *in general*, because if China and India, together accounting for a third of the world's population are excluded, there is no clear trend in inequality. This is not to say that changes in China and India do not matter – they are obviously of major importance – but it raises the question of whether their growth may be due to special circumstances. Though China has clearly opened up, it is still heavily controlled and far from the pure free-market paradigm. Possibly, China's success, which contrasts dramatically with the turmoil in Russia during the 1990s, indicates either the importance of the order in which reforms are introduced, or that there are other factors unique to China. The fact that liberalization of a very specific type has worked in China and India does not mean that it is a recipe for success everywhere, as is sometimes claimed.

A further problem with cross-country comparisons is that even if inequality between countries has fallen, during the same period inequality within countries has risen greatly. This is very marked in China and the United States (as well as in other countries, such as Britain). The rich have been pulling away, very fast, from the not-so rich. There is some evidence that the overall result may have been a rise in inequality, though problems with obtaining reliable data mean that there is a great deal of uncertainty attached to any estimates of the phenomenon.

EVALUATING GLOBALIZATION

Globalization makes a useful case study because it brings out several features that are common in economic argument. The first is that any answer to the question of whether globalization is good or bad *does* depend on the value judgements about the gains and losses experienced by different people. Irrespective of what has happened to inequality, it is undeniable that some people gain and others lose; hence, a position has to be taken on how to balance one person's gain against another's loss. This point is worth making because economists are often heard claiming that inter-personal comparisons of utility involve value judgements and so cannot be part of scientific economics. If economists took that to heart, the only view they could take, as economic scientists, on the merits of global-ization (or almost any other policy issue) would be that it depends on value judgments about which they can, as economists, say nothing. Yet they do not: many claim strongly that free trade and liberalization are beneficial. Sometimes it is argued that growth is beneficial because it gives the potential to raise everyone's welfare. Take the following remark by *Financial Times* columnist, Martin Wolf in an exchange with Robert Wade, professor of political economy and development at the LSE:

If a country's income rises rapidly, it does also possess greater means for improving the lot of the poor. Maybe the government refuses to use the opportunity, but a successor government could (Wolf and Wade, 2002).

This statement is correct. However, if the government does not use the opportunity to make sure that everyone is better off (which rarely happens), the only way we can conclude that this is an improvement is by judging that the benefits to the rich and the potential future benefits to the poor outweigh any losses the poor are now experiencing. That requires value judgements that go beyond those that economists are usu-ally prepared to endorse.

A second lesson from this case study is that it illustrates the complex-ity of what might seem a straightforward question – what are the effects of globalization on poverty and inequality? Measurement of poverty and inequality raises both conceptual and practical problems with the result that statistics are often subject to high levels of uncertainty and need to be treated with considerable caution. Theory also provides guidance but here, too, there are problems: because of the complexity of the problem, theories illustrate what might happen, taking certain factors into account and ignoring others. Some theories (static theories of competitive equi-librium or of comparative advantage) can be developed very formally, in comparison with which other theories (about stages of development or the sequencing of liberalization) are of necessity more informal and less complete. The result is that though theory and empirical work do constrain conclusions, the process through which this happens involves the application of judgement in weighing various types of evidence, not demonstrating something conclusively using a precise formal procedure, whether mathematical logic or arithmetic. Formal methods are needed but they can only confirm elements in the argument not the argument as a whole.

Finally, because of these difficulties, there is scope for economists' conclusions to be influenced by their goals and prior beliefs. Wade has pointed out that in the World Bank's *World Development Report 2000/2001: Attacking Poverty*, it was claimed that the number of people in poverty (under $1 per day) had risen from 1.18 to 1.2 billion, an increase of 20 million, from 1987 to 1998. Then came a report that claimed that the Bank was failing in its task because poverty had remained constant over this period and that its funding should be cut. The next significant World Bank publication, *Globalization, Growth and Poverty*, claimed that the poverty had fallen by 200 million from 1980 to 1998 (Wade 2004, p. 574). The suggestion is that the shift in emphasis could have been due to changing interests of the Bank (needing to show that it had made progress rather than that there was an important problem to be tackled) or to changing personnel who had different attitudes towards liberalization. The lesson here is *not* that there was deliberate distortion but that the margins of error were sufficiently large that it was possible for economists with different perspectives to draw opposing conclusions from substantially the same evidence.

Even statistics, which seem to be the 'hard' facts upon which interpretations are based, are 'softer' than they might appear to be. It is a problem that can arise when statistics are produced by an organization that is also responsible for policy. As Wade explains it,

Think of two models of a statistical organization that is part of a larger organization working on politically sensitive themes. The 'exogenous' model says that the statistics are produced by professionals exercising their best judgment in the face of difficulties that have no optimal solutions, who are managerially insulated from the overall tactical goals of the organization. The 'endogenous' models says that the statistics are produced by staff who act as agents of the senior managers (the principals), the senior managers expect them to help advance the tactical goals of the organization just like other staff, and the statistics staff therefore have to massage the data beyond the limits or professional integrity, or quit. (Wade 2004, pp. 583–4).

Wade goes on to remark that whilst the second view does *not* fit the World Bank, the Bank's commitment to an official view of how poverty should be reduced means that the first view does not fit it either. The statistical units in the Bank are partially insulated from the rest of the staff, but only partially. Stronger claims have been made about other organizations, such as one from a former IMF official, 'The managing director makes the big decisions, and the staff then puts together the numbers to justify them' (ibid.).

To repeat, the issue here is *not* fraud – it is that there is sufficient ambiguity in the figures and a sufficiently wide range of explanations that can be derived from those figures, that there is scope for disagreement. Perhaps the main complaint should be that economists are often too ready to draw specific conclusions rather than emphasize the uncertainty. Taking the above example, 20 million may sound a large number, but it is only 1.7% of the total poverty estimate and is probably well within the likely margin of error. In an ideal world, economists might simply declare the issue unresolved and wait for further data, but when urgent policy issues are at stake, and where the press is likely to ignore subtleties and qualifications, this hesitation is rarely politically possible, even though it may be justified by the lack of clear evidence.

It is often assumed that the beliefs or value judgements that influence economists' conclusions are ideological in the sense of being politically motivated. This is not necessarily the case. Of equal, if not greater, importance are beliefs about how science should operate and about what constitutes a persuasive argument. Faced with statistical evidence that is, on its own, not strong enough to provide compelling evidence for one theory of globalization, economists have to use other criteria to choose between competing explanations. They have formal theories of complete economies that are highly abstract and hence logically rigorous (notably, models of competitive general equilibrium). They also have rigorous theories about the elements of a problem, such as how people behave when there is incomplete information or the effects of a tariff on capital flows when markets are oligopolistic. And there are what might be called 'historical' theories that are not expressed or proved formally, of which arguments for protecting infant industries at a certain stage of historical development is a good example. The choice of any of these will depend as much on what the economist believes constitutes a convincing explanation as much as on his or her political beliefs. Often, of course, it may be hard to disentangle the two: certain types of theory may be favoured because they produce 'sensible' or 'plausible' conclusions, but what constitutes a 'sensible' or 'plausible' conclusion will rarely be precisely defined.

5

Money and Finance

The world of money and finance has been transformed almost beyond recognition in the past thirty years. As late as the 1970s, banks and other financial institutions were highly regulated, with little competition, and in many countries the movement of capital across international boundaries was tightly controlled. Many of these restrictions were swept away in a series of reforms, inaugurating a period of structural change and innovation. Nowhere was this more evident than in the City of London, one of the centres of the world financial system, where the 'Big Bang' of 27 October 1986, a set of reforms that changed overnight the regulations governing the way financial markets were organized, initiated enormous structural transformations, such as allowing banks to acquire stockbroking and market-making businesses. At the same time, new trading floors and the exploitation of modern technology transformed the way in which business was conducted. London became, in the view of many, the centre of the world's capital markets. But it was a London from which the old firms had disappeared and which was now dominated by American firms, with names like Goldman Sachs, Salomon Brothers, Morgan Stanley, Merrill Lynch, J. P. Morgan, and Lehman Brothers. London was becoming part of an international financial world in which geography was, for the most part, irrelevant.

It was not just the way financial institutions were organized that was transformed: the period starting in the early 1970s was one of ferocious financial innovation, with the creation of new financial assets too numerous to mention. These were made possible partly by new technology – the trading that could take place under the old regime, in a world where information travelled slowly and trades had to be registered using ledgers and pieces of paper, would, in essence, have been familiar to financiers a century or more earlier – and partly by the structural changes in the financial system that brought different activities together under the same roof or in the same organization. But this innovation was also made possible by developments in which economists played crucial roles. Theories developed by economists (and here the term has to be used inclusively because the boundary between the academic disciplines 'economics' and 'finance' is very blurred) were fundamental to many of the new financial products that had been created and which would, in the early twenty-first century, become so prominent. It also became necessary, in the new financial regime, for treasuries and central banks to reconsider their traditional views on policy making. Financial innovation had created a need for new approaches to regulation.

The academic theory of finance had begun to change, quite dramatically, with two papers, written in 1958 and 1961, by Franco Modigliani and Merton Miller, economists at the Graduate School of Industrial Administration at Carnegie Mellon University in Pittsburgh, Pennsylvania. Modigliani and Miller showed that in an ideal world firms would not care whether they funded their activities by raising equity finance (selling shares) or by borrowing (selling debt). Neither would it make any difference whether they retained their profits, thereby creating capital gains for their shareholders, or distributed them directly to shareholders as dividends. The details of the two Modigliani-Miller theorems, as they rapidly became known, are not important for the points being made here. What matters is that instead of the theory of finance being based on practitioners' beliefs and rules of thumb about the best practice to follow, theory began to be based on formal arguments about what rational, profit-seeking investors would do in a world in which they could freely buy and sell financial assets. Arbitrage – buying and selling assets so as to profit from prices being out of line with each other – was the key. In its pure form, arbitrage is completely without risk: if something, say a share, is being sold in two markets for different prices, then the arbitrageur can simultaneously buy in one market and sell in the other, achieving an instant, risk-free profit. The world necessary for the Modigliani-Miller theorems to hold may have been an ideal world that did not actually exist, but it was now possible to derive rigorous theorems about finance.

This new view, as it was already being called in the 1960s, was important, not just because it opened up the possibility of a scientific theory of finance, but also because it opened up the idea that steps should be taken to make the real world conform more closely to the ideal world of theory. The extent of this vision is made clear in a quotation from Fischer Black, one of the key figures in the story that follows:

In this [new] world, there will be no need for securities firms. Nonfinancial firms will issue their securities directly to investment firms. Individuals will adjust their borrowing and lending to match their spending needs, and will buy or sell shares of investment firms when they want to take more or less risk. Individuals will have no reason to own or trade in the shares of non-financial firms. (Mehrling 2005, p. 235)

The traditional view was that if investors wanted low risk, they invested in government stocks or shares in utilities such as gas and electricity, or even banks; these were unexciting and unlikely to yield large profits but they would yield a steady, reliable stream of interest or dividend income. Those wanting more risk would choose new industries or companies engaging in more speculative activity. But in the world Black described, risk was managed by financial companies, so that investors could be offered a much more varied and reliable menu of risk and return opportunities. It was this new world that created headlines in 2008.

ASSET PRICING AND DERIVATIVES TRADING

To understand this transformation in the theory and practice of finance, start with the problem of 'derivatives', which are financial assets the price of which depends on some other financial asset. Examples of derivatives include futures contracts (agreements to buy or sell assets at a future date) and options (the right to buy or sell an asset at a pre-agreed price, known respectively as 'call' and 'put' options). Since the early 1970s, trading in derivatives has grown enormously. In April 1973, when the Chicago Board Options Exchange opened, 911 options contracts were sold on the opening day. Three years later, 100,000 contracts a day were being concluded. At its peak, in 1987, daily volume was 700,000 contracts.

Over the following three decades many other types of derivative were developed, but options remain crucial because they direct attention to a particular problem, the packaging of risk.

Given that derivatives have existed for centuries, why did this 'boom' in the market happen at this particular time? Several factors are relevant. The instability of financial markets in the 1970s may have made investors more interested in securities that would reduce their exposure to risk than they had been in the post–Second World War 'golden age' of comparatively steady growth. Computer technology made it possible, for the first time, to perform the calculations necessary to work out appropriate prices sufficiently quickly for markets to operate properly. Perhaps more importantly, it was not until 1971, when the so-called Black-Scholes formula was derived, that traders knew how to calculate the value of options (and hence of many related types of derivative). Prior to this, those involved with options had used a variety of rules of thumb to decide how much options were worth, but there was no agreement on the right way to value them. The emergence of a large-scale options market required an agreed formula for working out their value.

The Black-Scholes formula, named after Fischer Black and Myron Scholes, was the outcome of academic research in finance which had, during the preceding decade, begun to transform the discipline of finance. This research was found in university economics departments, business schools and in the research departments of banks and other financial institutions, some of which had been set up by those who had developed the theories. Practitioners trying to figure out ways to make money did some of this work, but their research overlapped with work of a more traditional academic nature that investigated the implications of accepted theory and tried to explain empirical puzzles, such as the behaviour of stock prices.

The Black-Scholes formula was based on abstract, formal theorizing and grounded in assumptions with which economists were very familiar. Suppose we are considering the value of an option to purchase a share in the American Widget Corporation (AWC) for $10 at the end of the year. If AWC shares rise above $10, the holder of the option can purchase a share for $10 and sell it for an immediate profit. On the other hand, if shares end up selling for only $8, the holder of the option does nothing: the option lapses without any shares being purchased. Clearly, the option is valuable, depending on what is expected to happen to the price of AWC shares. If someone holds an option, they can make a profit if the share price rises, but they will not lose anything if the share price falls.

The insight underlying the Black–Scholes formula involves seeing that the value of an option to purchase shares is, given certain assumptions, equivalent to the value of an appropriate portfolio of shares and a risk-free asset. For example, consider an investor who holds 100 shares and the option to sell those shares (a put option) for a particular price (the exercise price). If the share price is high, the option is unlikely to be used, so its value will be low. On the other hand, if the share price is low, the option will be valuable because it is likely to be exercised. The value of the option will depend on the variability of the share price. This variability matters because an option will be more valuable for assets where there is more uncertainty about the price. If the price of a share is very predictable, an option will have little value, whereas if the share price fluctuates greatly, the insurance against price falls offered by a put option will be valuable.

Black and Scholes showed that changes in the price of an option and changes in the price of the underlying shares would exactly balance each other. This meant that buying shares together with a corresponding put option would yield a risk-free return. The final stage of the argument, proposed by Robert Merton, was to argue that if the market is efficient, this risk-free return must equal the return available on risk-free assets such as treasury bills. From this, it was possible to derive a formula linking the value of the option to the share price, the time before the option expired, its exercise price, the risk-free rate of interest and the variability of the share price.

The Black-Scholes formula was important because it provided what was seen as a legitimate way to attach a price to a wide variety of financial assets. The explanation in the previous paragraph related to the price of a put option, but it is equally applicable (mutatis mutandis) to call options (options to buy a share). It also turns out that many other financial assets have characteristics similar to options. Company shares, for example, can themselves be seen as options. If the value of a company falls too low, shareholders have the option to put the company into liquidation, forcing bondholders and other creditors to bear part of any loss. This is linked to the pricing of corporate bonds, becoming particularly important in the case of 'junk bonds', the term used to describe bonds issued by companies that have debts that are large in relation to their assets and where, as a result, the probability of default is high.

The growth of derivatives markets required more than just new ideas about finance. The law had to be changed so that trading in derivatives was not treated as gambling and ruled illegal. It also required new technology, for the creation of 'synthetic' assets required continually re-evaluating portfolios as prices changed. To see how this works, consider the relationship discussed above:

$$\text{Value of stock} + \text{value of put option on the stock}$$
$$= \text{Value of risk-free asset.}$$

Black and Scholes used this relationship to derive the value of a put option. However, it is also possible to mimic a put option by holding an appropriate combination of stock and risk-free assets: a synthetic put option. An investor wishing to hold a synthetic put observes the price of put options and holds a mixture of stock and cash (treasury bills) that changes as these prices change. As the stock price falls, the investor moves into cash. When the stock price reaches the floor (the equivalent of the exercise price on the option) the portfolio is entirely in cash. When the stock price rises, the portfolio is moved into stock. Synthetic put options are also known as dynamic portfolio insurance because insurance is provided by constantly moving the portfolio between stock and cash.

Alternatively, the relationship underlying the Black-Scholes formula can be rearranged as,

$$\text{Value of stock} = \text{value of risk-free asset} -$$
$$\text{value of put option on the stock.}$$

This means that, by holding a risk-free asset and short selling put options, it is possible to have a portfolio whose value behaves in exactly the same way as the prices of the underlying stocks. It is therefore possible, for example, to create a synthetic asset or derivative that exactly tracks the Standard and Poor's (S&P) 500 or the FTSE index or any other package of assets. The way to do this is to hold a suitable combination (which may involve short selling) of treasury bills and options on the S&P index or whatever security is being tracked.

The broader significance of these developments, and the reason why they proved so attractive to many investors, is that they make it possible to manage risk in a way that was not previously possible. Clearly, options and futures markets provide insurance for businesses that know they will have to buy or sell assets. More than that, they provide methods whereby investors in financial markets can alter the nature of the risks they face and, in some circumstances, increase the returns they obtain without being exposed to high levels of risk. This is important because if an investor wishes to diversify, it is important to find assets with returns that are not strongly correlated with each other. Most share prices are strongly correlated with the market as a whole. To reduce the overall risk of a portfolio it is therefore necessary to find assets (or synthetic assets) that are not correlated with the market index. Portfolio insurance, by insuring against movements in the stock-market index, makes it possible to construct a portfolio whose value does not vary with the stock market. This makes it the ideal vehicle for diversifying a portfolio.

Though finance was for a long time on the fringes of economics, the insights that led to the Black-Scholes formula arose directly out of economics. Central to Black-Scholes was the notion of arbitrage. If two prices were out of line with each other, there would be an opportunity for profit. Investors would sell the over-priced asset and buy the under-priced one, bringing prices into the appropriate relation with each other. It was because of arbitrage that the price of a stock/put-option combination must equal the price of the corresponding risk-free asset. Arbitrage, one of the dominant ideas in economics, lay at the heart of not simply the Black-Scholes formula but virtually all developments in the theory of finance since the late 1950s. It is an economic rather than a mathematical argument. Furthermore, though several of those working on the modern theory of finance faced opposition in that prominent economists and journals claimed that this work was not really economics, it in fact arose from the heart of the economics profession – notably the economics departments and business schools of the University of Chicago and MIT.

The Black-Scholes formula created potential markets for many new financial assets: trading in risk could be divorced from trading in the real assets that ultimately lay behind the financial assets. For example, buying an asset linked to the Dow Jones or the FTSE index made it possible to benefit from share prices without owning any specific shares. It all rested on the legitimacy of the formula on which valuations were made. However, to say this is not to say that the Black-Scholes formula was correct; it was known that it was an approximation, and that departures from it could be significant under certain circumstances. The formula was important because without it, not only would traders not have known how to value assets, but they would also have been unable to evaluate decisions that other traders were making. There is, therefore, a sense in which the formula worked because those involved in financial markets believed in it.

An early and dramatic sign of the problems that could arise in this new world of finance came on 19 October 1987, when stock markets across the world fell by almost 25 per cent in a single day. One of the causes of this enormous fall in share prices was portfolio insurance and computer-driven trading. As share prices started to fall, dynamic hedging required that investors move into cash: they had to sell shares, pushing prices downwards. Thus, price falls led automatically to increased sales and hence to further price falls. But prices were falling so rapidly that it was not always possible to sell at the current market price, and models based on being able instantly to sell at this price did not work. Strategies that might have worked when this type of trading was negligible in relation to the market as a whole did not work when 'insured' portfolios accounted for 3 per cent of the market.

LONG-TERM CAPITAL MANAGEMENT

A concrete illustration of what happened when these ideas were put into practice is offered by Long-Term Capital Management (LTCM), a hedge fund set up in 1994, whose partners included Scholes and Merton, who went on to win the Nobel memorial prize in economics for 1997 for their work on derivatives pricing (Fischer Black had died in 1995, and the prize is never awarded posthumously). The firm engaged in a variety of arbitrage strategies. One involved buying long-term, often high-risk, debt and the short selling (equivalent to negative holdings) of safe short-term bonds. This combination of investments insured them against general movements in interest rates and was considered low-risk. Another strategy involved taking long positions (buying shares) in firms that were likely to be taken over and short positions (negative holdings) in would-be purchasers of those companies. This was also a low-risk strategy: it insured them against general movements in stock prices (losses on long positions would be offset by gains on short positions). Profits were to be made from movement in relative prices: from long bonds becoming safer as their term fell, and from the price of takeover candidates rising relative to that of the firms taking them over.

These low-risk strategies typically yielded low returns. LTCM overcame this by leverage – using borrowed funds. Suppose a firm can make 4 per cent return on its assets. If it has a capital of $1 million and borrows $99 million, its total assets are $100 million, which means it makes a profit of $4 million. If it can borrow at 3 per cent, interest payments account for almost $3 million, leaving a net return of $1 million – a rate of return of 100 per cent on the firm's capital. The downside is that leverage also magnifies losses, so that if, in the above example, the firm made 2 per cent instead of 4 percent, its capital would be completely wiped out. For this reason, leverage (the ratio of debt to equity) was traditionally limited to around 2:1, or sometimes 4:1. However, because of the high reputation of its partners (including the two Nobel Prize winners) and what were perceived to be very conservative investment strategies, LTCM managed to have leverage ratios of the order of 25:1 or 30:1. On top of this, LTCM engaged heavily in various types of derivatives trading.

For several years, LTCM's investment strategy was vindicated. Returns were 20 percent in 1994; 40 per cent in 1995–6; and 17 per cent in 1997. However, in August 1998. LTCM came unstuck when Russia announced that it could no longer pay the interest on its debts. LTCM had invested heavily in Russian bonds, the value of which plummeted. The gamble had been that, with the coming of the Euro, European interest rates would fall relative to U.S. rates, but with the Russian default the reverse happened. These events fed through into the U.S. stock market, where prices became much more volatile. Options became more expensive and investors tried to substitute dynamic hedging, increasing volatility. The effect on LTCM's positions was disastrous. By mid-September, its balance sheet had shrunk from $125 billion to $100 billion, but its capital had fallen from $2.5 billion to $600 million, raising its leverage to more than 150:1. On September 23, 1998 a group of sixteen financial institutions took over 90 percent of LTCM's assets. Though the fund continued after that under new managers, the original venture was effectively over.

Was this episode a success for financial economics? In one sense, the answer is clearly 'Yes'. Economic principles, notably the ideas of arbitrage and efficient markets, were used to open up and exploit financial markets. LTCM made enormous profits, adding to the wealth of those involved. But what does the downfall of LTCM show? The obvious answer is to say that it points to the effects of chance. With risky strategies, it is normal to win some gambles and lose others. LTCM had a run of good luck followed by some bad luck. This answer implies that it would be wrong to attach too much significance either to the years when things were going well or to the collapse – perhaps it *was* no more than a run of good luck followed by some bad luck. In LTCM's calculations, the market movements that undermined their positions were extremely unlikely events. This can be read two ways. Either the firm was extremely unlucky, or there was something wrong with the model on which risk assessments were based.

It could be argued that economic ideas showed that there were profitable opportunities available to be exploited and that the money made by LTCM (and other hedge funds) proved that the theory was correct. The fact that there were risks involved does not undermine this claim. However, the LTCM affair points rather clearly to limitations in the economic theory. To understand this, it is necessary to understand why the portfolio insurance strategy, which should have protected portfolios against losses, failed. There are two problems here. The first, already discussed briefly in the context of the 1987 crash, is that portfolio insurance involves selling equities when share prices are falling. If one firm sells, and it is a small market participant whose behaviour does not affect other traders, there is no problem with this strategy. There is, however, a problem when many firms start behaving in this way, because selling shares pushes downward pressure on share prices, triggering further sales. This is an unstable situation and could have contributed to the rise in the volatility of the stock market during the 1990s. The second is that the portfolio insurance strategy presumes that markets are 'thick', that it is always possible to buy and sell at the current price. In times of rapidly changing prices, including financial panics, it is possible that there may be no one wishing to buy. If firms are programmed to sell automatically, the result may be enormous falls in share prices (such as happened on October 19, 1987) that make it impossible to maintain desired portfolios without making large losses.

This shows that, for many purposes, financial markets can be considered efficient, and that conclusions can be drawn from the assumption that arbitrage will prevent the emergence of disparities in security prices. However, when it comes to designing policies that affect the way the whole system works, the assumption that traders are price takers in efficient, competitive markets cannot be taken for granted. Under these circumstances, arbitrage-based finance theory may not yield the best guidance. It may be necessary to take into account the social and psychological aspects of the way market participants respond to new information, the route taken by what has come to be called 'behavioural economics'.

MONETARY POLICY – THE UK EXAMPLE

Financial innovation and the liberalization of financial markets transformed the environment in which monetary policy had to operate. Though this change was worldwide (Ben Bernanke, who later succeeded Alan Greenspan as chairman of the U.S. Federal Reserve, claimed that by 1997, some form of inflation targeting was also being pursued in Canada, New Zealand, Sweden, Australia, Finland, Spain and Israel), it can be illustrated with developments in the United Kingdom. Between 1970 and 1997, there were many changes in UK monetary policy. To understand how these evolved, it is useful to start with the new system, 'Competition and Credit Control', which was introduced in 1971. This new policy aimed at freeing up the monetary system to make it more competitive and, it was hoped, more efficient.

To understand how competition and credit control were intended to work, it is necessary to understand how banks make money. Typically a bank borrows short and lends long: it receives deposits or borrows in short-term money markets, and either lends to customers or buys long-term debt. The reason this is profitable is that deposits and short-term debt normally carry lower rates of interest than loans or long-term debt. Because their borrowing is short-term, banks need to hold reserves of cash or assets that can quickly be turned into cash so that they are always in a position to repay money to depositors. Holding high reserves makes a bank safer, but this has to be balanced against the cost because reserves (safe, short-term assets) carry lower rates of interest than the bank could make on riskier investments. The problem for regulators, in this case the Bank of England, is ensuring that banks are sufficiently safe without exerting excessive control over their operations.

Under the old regime the commercial banks had been subject to a range of controls on their activities covering types of lending they were allowed to undertake and the conditions under which they were allowed to lend. These regulations were designed both to ensure that banks were safe and that the Bank of England could control the volume of lending, and hence the amount of spending in the economy. Competition and Credit Control sought to replace such regulations with a system of control that operated only through reserve requirements: provided that banks held certain proportions of their deposits in various types of safe short-term asset, they could borrow and lend freely. However, this immediately proved inadequate. In 1972–3 what is known as 'broad money' (defined as currency in circulation plus a wide range of bank deposits) grew at about 25 per cent per annum. New measures, dubbed the 'corset' because they were designed to prevent the money supply from rising too much, were introduced. The corset meant that if banks' lending increased too much, they had to make additional deposits with the Bank of England, on which they received no interest. This was not particularly effective in reducing inflationary pressures, however, mainly because banks were able to move business offshore (outside the United Kingdom), where the regulations did not apply. In the face of rising world inflation and the oil-price rises of 1973–4, the high growth rate of the money supply was probably an important reason why UK inflation rose even more than inflation in most other developed countries. It peaked at 24 per cent (in 1975) compared with 11 per cent in the United States and 13 per cent for industrial countries as a whole.

Faced with this inflation and a balance of payments crisis in 1976, the government turned to monetary control, along with incomes policy (an agreement with the trade unions to limit wage rises) and large cuts in government spending. The monetary regime changed to one in which, partly to meet conditions laid down by the IMF, a target was set for monetary growth. Inflation fell dramatically for two years, but as the general election approached in 1979, monetary policy became freer and real interest rates (interest rates adjusted for inflation) fell as the government allowed spending and inflation to rise. By the middle of 1980, inflation was back at 20 per cent per annum.

The incoming Conservative government was committed to reducing inflation by controlling the growth rate of the money supply, and real interest rates were raised sharply from the end of 1979. Even though what was considered the most important monetary aggregate (Sterling M3) continued to rise rapidly, the result was a dramatic rise in the exchange rate. The real exchange rate (taking account of changes in UK labour costs relative to those in the rest of the world) rose by 50 per cent in less than two years, a rise unparalleled in other industrial countries. Output in manufacturing, the sector most exposed to foreign competition and least able to cope with this loss in competitiveness, fell by 12 per cent in eighteen months. The 1981 recession was, after that of 1974, the worst since the Great Depression. Other factors were involved, in particular the advent of North Sea oil production and the 1979 oil-price rise, but monetary policy was clearly a major factor.

During the 1980s, monetary policy remained high on the political agenda. In the interests of encouraging free markets, the incoming government removed the corset and controls on foreign exchange. Over the next few years they set well-publicized targets for the growth of £M3 in the hope that this would lower expectations of inflation and that this would feed through into a fall in inflation. However, they consistently failed to hit these targets. They contemplated introducing new mechanisms of monetary control, such as monetary base control – controlling the supply of bank reserves, in order to achieve their targets. Instead, targets were modified to take into account a broader range of monetary indicators. In part, this was inevitable; financial liberalization, in the United Kingdom and elsewhere, was making it far easier for investors to shift funds from one asset to another. If one group of deposits were controlled, it would be possible to create substitutes that were not controlled. The situation thus changed from one where targets were not credible (because they were never hit) to one where targets were not sufficiently precise for the markets to know whether they had been met or not.

In the later 1980s and early 1990s, monetary policy became tied up with the issue of sterling's relationship with the emerging European Monetary System (EMS). There was a period in 1987 when the government 'shadowed' the German mark, using interest rates for this purpose. Shortly afterwards there was the period, from 1990–2, when the United Kingdom entered the EMS, and interest rates were driven by the need to peg the exchange rate within the allowable bands. This was a disaster. Perhaps influenced by electoral considerations, perhaps by fears of a world slump after the 1987 stock market crash, the government kept UK interest rates too low, contributing to inflation and an unsustainable rise in the level of activity. The boom collapsed in 1991, resulting in a third major post-war recession. This period was also disastrous for the EMS, under strain because of the financial effects of German reunification, and it ended with the UK's abrupt departure in 1992.

These events formed the backdrop for the new policy regime introduced by the incoming Labour government in 1997. Monetary policy had clearly failed to achieve the objectives set for it over the previous two decades. Admittedly, there had been large shocks and errors in other areas of policy, but it is clear that the monetary policy regime had not coped well, and there was considerable evidence that monetary policy had been a source of problems. Above all, the operation of monetary policy had become highly politicized, every change in interest rates being made with a view to the political as well as the economic consequences. To give more stability to monetary policy and to ensure some consistency, it made sense to distance it from the political arena and to change the way in which it was conducted.

The new regime involved two key elements: (1) moving towards a formal target for the inflation rate; and (2) establishing the operational independence of the Bank of England. Legislation was passed requiring the government to set an annual target for inflation, which initially was 2.5 per cent per annum. The Bank of England had the task of keeping inflation within a band of 1 percentage point on either side of this target. To accomplish this, a new institution, the Monetary Policy Committee (MPC), was created, which met monthly and included not only Bank of England officials but also independent experts (economists). The MPC would use forecasts and any information it considered relevant to set interest rates, with the sole objective of meeting the inflation target set by the government. Transparency was to be ensured by publication of regular inflation reports and, shortly after each meeting, the minutes and voting record of the MPC. A clear policy was set out describing the consequences of not hitting the target.

At the same time, the responsibility for the stability of the financial system was taken away from the Bank of England and passed to the newly created Financial Services Authority (FSA). Establishing a regulatory regime was considered a separate problem from using interest rates and other operations in financial markets aimed at controlling inflation. This move was intended to clarify the regime; under the old system, bank reserve requirements (the level of cash and other short-term liquid assets they needed to hold) were both a device to ensure that banks were always in a position to meet their obligations and a way to regulate their activities, hence controlling the volume of bank deposits in the economy. Under the new regime they lost the latter role.

The regulatory regime established in 1997, though it may be more formal, has much in common with regimes established in other countries and reflects best practices as recommended in much of the academic literature. Earlier, the emphasis had been on analysing the effects of policy changes (what happens if government spending rises by £1 million or if the rate of interest is raised from 5% to 6%). With the advent of the new approach to macroeconomics that emerged in the 1970s (see Chapter 7), however, the emphasis shifted towards analysing policy regimes, or the rules by which policy decisions were taken (e.g., how would the authorities respond if unemployment or inflation changed). The 1997 regime involved setting out clear policy rules; their implementation was treated as a technical matter. Along with this went an interest in ruling out monetary policy surprises. The publication of the information available to the MPC and its voting record was designed to minimize the element of surprise. For example, even if the MPC did not change interest rates, the voting record might indicate whether the vote had been unanimous in favour of not changing interest rates or whether it had been a majority decision, enabling observers to assess the likelihood of a change the following month. This importance given to predictability was arguably the result of economists' emphasizing the disturbing effects of unanticipated policy changes.

Even more important, the system was designed to achieve credibility. A large economics literature argued that monetary policy could achieve changes in inflation at much lower cost if the public believed that announced policies would be carried through. Suppose, for example, that the government announces that it is going to reduce inflation using monetary policy (interest rates). The theory suggested that if the public believed that inflation would fall, the effects on output and unemployment would be much smaller than if the public were sceptical about whether the policy would actually be carried out. It can thus be argued that the system was designed in response to ideas that had emerged directly from the macroeconomic literature of the preceding two decades. Focusing on inflation was also consistent with the new macroeconomic theories that emerged in the 1970s because in these models changes in inflation were seen to be closely linked to changes in output and employment.

The regime was also consistent with the view that finance was a field where, provided that macroeconomic stability was not threatened, private-sector financial institutions should be allowed to conduct their affairs without excessive regulation. Innovation was to be encouraged. The separation of monetary economics and finance is echoed in the literature, wherein comparatively few economists constructed models linking them. (An article by Bernanke [1981] on the importance of credit for the level of economic activity was an exception; but, though he was apparently prescient in seeing the importance of bankruptcy, even his work failed to explore fully the macroeconomic implications of financial sector organisation.) Finance was a means of making economic activity more efficient, and financial policy was concerned with the stability of individual institutions, whereas monetary policy was about macroeconomic stability. People should be allowed to speculate in risky investments, bearing the consequences of their actions. The result was that the Bank of England was unable to raise interest rates to counter speculative booms in share prices or the housing market, even though it saw potential dangers emerging. All the Governor of the Bank of England, Mervyn King, could do was to issue careful warnings, which were meant to be strong enough to be taken seriously, without causing alarm, in the hope that he could gradually push expectations downwards.

It is also worth noting that the MPC essentially gave economists from business and academia, together with Bank of England officials (some of whom were economists) responsibility for achieving the target. Politicians were involved in setting the target, but once it had been set, they had no further role. This was the meaning of operational independence. Thus the task of assessing what was going on in the economy, anticipating what was going to affect inflation in the near future, and how the economy would respond to any change in interest rates, was left to economists. Although economic advice had previously always been sought, and the Bank of England had always had a powerful voice, the final decision had previously rested with a political figure.

For the first few years, the system appeared to be successful in that there followed almost a decade of remarkably steady growth, low and stable inflation, and falling unemployment. When comparison was made with earlier decades, it appeared that, at last, the problem of monetary policy had been solved, a tribute both to those who operated the system and to the economic ideas on which it was based. However, it is highly significant that this improvement in economic performance took place at a time when the world economy was experiencing what, after the mildness of the 2001 recession became apparent, came to be called 'the great moderation'. Given the importance of external events to the UK economy, its stability cannot be attributed to UK policy alone. Of course, insofar as the great moderation reflected a shared wisdom amongst key policy makers the world over, it is possible that it should be attributed to the policy regime.

If estimates are to be believed, a one percentage point change in the interest rate set by the bank produces a change in inflation of only a third or a quarter percentage point. Since interest rates changed no more than four percentage points for the first few years of the MPC's existence, the direct effect of its actions cannot have been more than one percentage point. Thus if the new regime was the cause of stability, it must have had an effect on expectations, thus altering the behaviour of economic agents. If people believed that the MPC would do whatever was needed to hit its inflation target, this expectation could become self-fulfilling, without the need for major actions by the MPC. As for recent policy changes, they are best subsumed into a discussion of the worldwide crisis of 2007–8.

THE 2007–8 CREDIT CRUNCH

On 9 August 2007, the French bank BNP Paribas announced that it was suspending withdrawals from three of its investment funds because it had decided that it was no longer able to value loans that were ultimately backed by sub-prime mortgages in the United States. These were loans that had been made to enable people with limited or irregular incomes to purchase homes. When interest rates had been low, these households could maintain their payments, but over the preceding three years interest rates had risen dramatically, pushing up the rate of default. In their efforts to manage risk, mortgage lenders had begun re-packaging these mortgages (passing them on to other institutions). These packages of mortgages had then been repackaged into further assets, with different levels of risk, that were then sold on to other financial institutions. Statistical models were used to assess risk, but these calculations allowed only for individual risks (the risks that certain households would default), not for the problems emerging in the system as a whole. This was not the first sign of a crisis, which had already affected the U.S. investment bank, Bear Stearns, but it indicated that the crisis was becoming global, and the short-term credit markets on which the major banks relied were seizing up.

The European Central Bank, the Federal Reserve and the Bank of Japan all responded by making additional credit available, and interest rates were cut, but this did not solve the problem of credit drying up. The rate at which banks lent to each other rose significantly, reflecting the shortage of funds, and on 13 September 2007, a British Bank, Northern Rock, was forced to go to the Bank of England for support, a move that resulted, the following February, in its nationalization. More than other mortgage lenders, Northern Rock had relied heavily on being able to raise funds in the money markets, enabling it to expand its lending far in excess of the funds it raised from depositors. Over the following months, despite further attempts by central banks to increase the flow of credit, it became clear that losses were spreading throughout the financial system, encompassing not only banks, but also the companies that provided the insurance that was meant to convert risky assets into safe ones.

As the crisis spread during 2008, with falling house prices in the United States and Europe causing more households to default on their mortgages, banks began to fail, most being taken over by rivals for a fraction of what they had been worth only a few months before. In the United States, the casualties among the investment banks included Bear Stearns, which was taken over by J. P. Morgan Chase; Merrill Lynch, which was bought by Bank of America, and Lehman Brothers, which filed for bankruptcy. Among commercial banks, Wachovia was taken over by Wells Fargo. The U.S. government effectively took over two of the largest mortgage lenders and its biggest insurer, American International Group (AIG). In the United Kingdom, the government brokered a deal whereby a major bank, Halifax Bank of Scotland (HBOS), was taken over by a larger bank, Lloyds TSB, but when the scale of HBOS's exposure to bad debts was uncovered, Lloyds TSB had to turn to the government for support. In the Eurozone, a series of banks and insurance companies had to be nationalized or bailed out.

Governments had been desperate to prevent the major banks from collapsing because collapse would have caused economic activity to come to an abrupt halt as customers suddenly found that they could not get hold of cash. Bernanke, at the Federal Reserve, whose academic career had involved research on the Great Depression, was acutely aware that the collapse of the banking system had been a major reason the Depression had been so severe. The downturn therefore led him, once the extent of the crisis had become clear, to respond by aggressively reducing interest rates to almost zero, accompanying this with injections of credit, a policy followed later by the Bank of England. However, during 2008 it became clear that a shortage of credit and falling demand as consumers tried to build up their assets were going to result in a significant depression. In June 2009, General Motors, once the icon of American industry, filed for bankruptcy protection, before it was restructured with government support. Initial hopes that the financial crisis and fall in the stock market would have little effect on the real economy, as had been the case in 2001–2 after the collapse of the 'dot-com' bubble, rapidly evaporated. The United States entered a recession, according to the National Bureau of Economic Research (NBER) definition of two quarters of negative growth, at the end of 2008, and it became clear that such problems would be worldwide. The only questions concerned the optimal policy response and how quickly it would end.

THE THEORY OF MONEY AND FINANCE IN ACTION

Clearly, these events, from the new financial markets that were introduced in the 1970s to the crisis of 2007–8 and the responses of policy makers were the result of political and social changes that extended far beyond the discipline of economics. However, whilst the outcomes will, equally clearly, have reflected the way ideas were taken up and put into practice, it is possible to draw conclusions about how economics fared. The most important point is that, despite recent problems, there is an important sense in which the modern theory of finance worked: many people, including some of the economists who created the theory, used it to transform financial markets and to become very wealthy. Financial products based on the new theories of finance were created and traded and in the eyes of many became an indispensable aspect of business, enabling firms to raise funds in new ways and to manage the risks to which they are exposed. Part of the reason the theory worked must clearly be that most of those involved in financial markets are trying to make money and take advantage of opportunities that present themselves (the essence of the arbitrage that is the foundation on which modern financial theory, from the Modigliani-Miller theorems to option-pricing theory, is based), and that the theory deals with assets having clearly defined properties that can be modelled precisely. Yet, for the theory to work, the world had to change. In addition to the necessary changes in regulations governing the financial system and advances in information technology, it was also important that traders believed the models and began to behave in such a way that the formulae for valuing financial assets worked. If traders had not believed it, the theory could not have worked.

Economic arguments go part of the way towards answering the Queen's question, with which Chapter 1 opened, about why no one predicted the crisis. It is impossible to predict a stock market collapse; if it were predictable, people would already have predicted it and as a result it would have happened already. However, that is only part of the story. Whilst it may be impossible to forecast *precisely* when the collapse will occur, there were many economists who did see that something was seriously wrong: they anticipated that a crash was virtually inevitable at some point, though they could not tell either when it would come, or how serious it would be.

However, though at one level the theory worked, when it came to assessing the wider consequences of financial innovation, the theory failed. The theory of finance was based on the claim that markets were efficient. Although there was some evidence to the contrary, most finance specialists chose to believe that the assumption of efficient markets was good enough. The result was that economists (with some notable exceptions) failed to take account of the implications of financial innovation for the economy as a whole. At a forum organized by the British Academy to find an answer to the Queen's question, involving thirty-three prominent economists and public figures, Tim Besley and Peter Hennessy, reporting on the conclusions reached, claimed that failure to see the crisis coming 'was principally a failure of the collective imagination of many bright people, both in this country and internationally, to understand the risks to the system as a whole' (http://www.britac.ac.uk/events/archive/forum-economy.cfm, accessed on 19 February 2010). This judgement, however, understates the problem. For the 'failure of the collective imagination' was directly encouraged by theories that presented a distinctly Panglossian view of the world. That managers might deal in assets they did not understand to an extent that jeopardized not only the firms for which they worked but also the financial system as a whole, or that the system might be too fragile to survive without massive intervention by the authorities were apparently never considered.

Just as in the case of the Russian transition from socialism to capitalism, discussed in Chapter 3, the practical consequences of economic reasoning are hard to disentangle from politics and 'failings' of individuals. When profits and earnings were high, it was difficult to spoil the party. Accounts of the period are full of instances of people suspecting that something was wrong but either not being listened to or holding back their doubts. There was also a reluctance to recognize some of the risks that were being taken. Gillian Tett (2009) provides a clear illustration of this. The bankers at J. P. Morgan, who had created many of the products that turned sour in 2007–8, and who were experienced in risk management, could not work out how their competitors were making so much money through trading that, on J. P. Morgan's calculations, was not profitable. It was only when the crisis hit and those banks were in trouble that it occurred to them that their rivals had been oblivious to the risks to which they were exposed. As long as there was prosperity, it was easy to dismiss warnings such as those of Paul Krugman about 'the return of depression economics', Joseph Stiglitz's claim that the stock market expansion contained 'the seeds of its own destruction', or Robert Shiller's analysis of 'irrational exuberance' (a phrase taken from Alan Greenspan). Their authors could be dismissed as Cassandras, ideologically motivated or lacking faith in free enterprise. (Krugman, for example, had developed a public profile as a strong critic of the Bush administration, making it easier to dismiss his economic analysis as ideologically driven.)

Economists have clearly learned much about monetary policy since the 1970s: they could hardly have failed to have done so given the turbulence and challenges that policy makers have faced. In Britain and many other countries, a broad, though not universal consensus emerged during the 1990s in which a commitment to low inflation was combined with a pragmatic approach to achieving it that focused on interest rates. Setting a target for inflation itself reflected a belief that employment and productivity were best tackled using other policy instruments or left to the market. The separation of monetary policy from supervision of the financial system, which proved such a severe problem in 2007–8, was

justified by policy makers as a workable division of labour that would
permit the Bank of England and the FSA to focus on specialized tasks.
It was a problem that arguably should have been raised by economists,
but finance did not appear in the models used to understand how policy
rules might work.

It is possible to argue that economists failed to see the problems that
emerged because of blindness caused by their commitment to the model
of rational choice. However, it should be noted that even insiders, such
as those at J. P. Morgan, who were instrumental in creating derivatives,
could not conceive that other banks were taking absurd risks – they took
it for granted that their competitors must be monitoring their exposure
to risk: it would be irrational not to do so. To observe that the way managers were remunerated may have made it perfectly rational for them
to focus on short-term returns, even if this meant pursuing strategies
that could potentially bankrupt their companies, is only a partial answer
because it begs the question of why remuneration contracts took the
form that they did.

The 2007–8 crisis has also raised serious questions about the role of
macroeconomic theory – the theories that lay behind a monetary policy
regime that was centred on using interest rates to achieve inflation targets.
It is probably fair to say that the crisis, insofar as it could be anticipated,
was anticipated by only a minority of economists. Many economists were
clearly taken by surprise and forced to re-think their position. The rest
were probably aware of potential problems that were emerging (notably,
rising property and share prices and increased indebtedness), and they
even possessed the tools to analyse them, but they failed to realize how
important these problems would become or how soon a crisis would
happen. This can be explained in part, no doubt, by the reason mentioned above, that in a time of prosperity, there is great reluctance to
listen to those who claim that rising wealth is based on a house of cards
that will eventually collapse. However, as macroeconomic theory is covered in more detail in Chapter 7, discussion of its role in the crisis is best
postponed to that point.

PART II

HISTORICAL PERSPECTIVES

It is possible to draw some limited conclusions from the examples of economics in action discussed in Part I. It would be wrong either to dismiss economics altogether (the discipline clearly has some successes to its credit) or to sweep such concerns aside (there are reasons to believe it may have played a significant role in some major disasters). It also seems clear that economics is most successful where problems are narrowly defined and that its application is most problematic when wider issues, involving politics or social phenomena, need to be considered. Neither of these conclusions should be at all surprising, though it is surprising how often commentators focus on one and ignore the other.

To understand what is going on in economics – to see the bigger picture behind these case studies – it is necessary to delve a little deeper, for understanding this bigger picture involves trying to understand why economists think as they do. It is otherwise impossible to understand the disagreements that persist in the subject. To do this, we need to look into its recent history. A good place to start is with economists' definitions of economics. Although such definitions may not describe what economists actually do, they reveal much about the way they understand what they are doing. Chapter 6 explores this through discussing the question of what it means to be scientific, for this perspective reveals economists' views on what constitutes a good argument within their discipline. That leads naturally into Chapter 7, on the attempt to construct scientific theories of how the economy as a whole works: the search for a rigorous macroeconomics. After that, we turn to the problems of ideology (Chapter 8) and dissent (Chapter 9) within economics. In all cases, though, these discussions have a much longer history, attention is focused on the era since the Second World War (with a few incursions into the 1930s). For this is when modern ideas on economics were shaped.

6

Creating a 'Scientific' Economics

ECONOMIC SCIENCE

When the Econometric Society was founded in 1930 to promote mathematical and statistical work in economics, its constitution echoed a new view of what it meant to be scientific:

> Its main object shall be to promote studies that aim at a unification of the theoretical-quantitative and the empirical-quantitative approach to economic problems and that are penetrated by constructive and rigorous thinking similar to that which has come to dominate in the natural sciences. (http://www.econometricsociety.org/society.asp#constitution, accessed on 20 February 2010)

For the creators of the Econometric Society, to be scientific was to derive results rigorously, using mathematical methods to achieve greater rigour than would be possible using verbal analysis. Scientific rigour meant logical rigour, dictating that the economics be concerned with developing and analysing precisely specified mathematical models. Rigour in economic theory therefore meant simplifying problems so that they could be formulated as sets of equations, which could then be manipulated using suitable mathematical techniques. Propositions in economic theory could thus be as rigorous as the mathematical techniques that were employed. The assumptions might be arbitrary and abstract, but the results derived from them were rigorous.

This was very different from the view held by many economists, especially in the United States, in the interwar period, when scientific rigour meant ensuring that scientific theories were firmly rooted in the real world. For this earlier generation,

Being scientific meant devoting time and resources to the production of much more, and more reliable, economic observations and quantitative data; taking a view of theories as tentative, stating theories and hypotheses in a form that permitted them to be subject to examination and test on the basis of empirical observations, including statistical analysis and experimental tests; being dispassionate and, as far as possible, free from ideological bias; using behavioural or motivational premises consistent with the state of scientific knowledge in related fields, particularly psychology; and creating knowledge useful for solving concrete problems. (Rutherford 1999, p. 236)

From the 1930s onwards, the Econometric Society's conception of what it meant to be rigorous became increasingly influential. Economics came to be seen as a technical discipline centred on modelling – the construction of mathematical representations of the economic activity.

This shift reflected changes in the concept of rigour in the natural sciences. For the great applied mathematicians of the early twentieth century, such as Henri Poincaré and Albert Einstein, rigour meant basing one's mathematical modelling directly on experimental results. To be rigorous meant to be constrained by empirical data. However, partly in response to the superseding of classical physics with the theory of relativity and quantum mechanics, rigour instead came to be associated with formal reasoning in science and in mathematics. Modelling was about establishing the logical consistency of theories, rather than establishing firm links between theories and data.

The question of method was implicitly linked to the question of what economics was. Economics had traditionally been defined in terms of its subject matter as 'the study of wealth', 'the study of the business system' or, in the words of Alfred Marshall, a Cambridge economist and the author of the leading economics textbook in the early twentieth century, as 'the study of mankind in the ordinary business of life'. Given such definitions, it was not clear that economics was a field that could be studied with a high level of mathematical rigour. Mathematics played a role, but a limited one, symbolized by Marshall's refusal, in his *Principles of Economics* (1920) to allow mathematics into the main text (it was confined to footnotes and appendices). However, there was another view of what economics was that focused on 'economizing' as the essential feature of economic activity. Drawing on that tradition, Lionel Robbins at the LSE came up with a definition of economics that was much more congenial to the creation of a rigorous economic theory. In *An Essay on the Nature and Significance of Economic Science* (1932), Robbins offered what eventually came to be the most widely discussed definition of economics:

Economics is the science which studies human behaviour as a relationship between ends and scarce means which have alternative uses. (Robbins 1932, p. 15)

Robbins minimized the novelty of his definition, but it had radical implications. Although Robbins himself was not an enthusiast for mathematical economics, and was not one of the founders of the Econometric Society, his definition suggested that rigorous mathematical methods could be at the heart of economics. For economic science was about working out the implications of the need for choice under conditions of scarcity. Making the best use of scarce resources led directly to the notion that economics was about optimization; hence, that the methods of differential calculus could be used. Because it was, unlike previous 'classificatory' definitions that identified the subject-matter of economics, an 'analytical' definition, another implication was that economics defined an *aspect* of behaviour, with the result that 'any kind of human behaviour falls within the scope of Economic Generalisations. … There are no limitations on the subject-matter of Economic Science save this' (Robbins 1932, p. 16).

Though economists sometimes talk as though this is *the* definition of economics, it took about thirty years for it to be widely accepted, and even then, some very prominent economists rejected it. Textbooks continued to use more traditional definitions, and when the definition was discussed in academic journals, it was usually to criticize it as either too broad (covering almost any aspect of human behaviour, including, for example, political processes) or too narrow (the problem of unemployment was about unused resources, not scarcity), and biased towards economic theory and against historical and empirical research. It was not until the early 1960s that the Robbins definition gained wide acceptance. This was no coincidence. This period, from the 1930s to the 1960s, was exactly when economics became a predominantly mathematical discipline.

The trend towards seeing economics as a technical mathematical discipline was greatly accelerated by the Second World War, when many economists entered government service, working on problems related to the war effort. Obviously, economists were employed in agencies such as the Federal Trade Commission, the Treasury and the Office of Price Administration. But they were also employed, as were many social scientists, in bodies involved more directly with military activity, such as the Office of Strategic Services (OSS), the forerunner of the Central Intelligence Agency (CIA). There, they were employed as general problem solvers, working alongside not only fellow social scientists, but also mathematicians, physicists and engineers. They helped to provide intelligence on German and Japanese military capacity and to assess the economic impact of Allied bombing. But they also became involved in what had come to be called Operations Research (OR), solving problems such as quality control in shell manufacture or the design of aircraft gun-sights. It was an interdisciplinary environment, spanning the natural and the social sciences, focusing on problems of resource use and allocation and conducive to the development and application of mathematical techniques. At the end of the war, U.S. higher education expanded rapidly, and economists with wartime experience in government, many of whom were far more mathematically oriented than were their typical counterparts before the war, rapidly became influential figures in the discipline.

In the 1940s and 1950s, the clearest endorsements of the Robbins definition came from members of the Cowles Commission. This was a research institute established in 1932 by a businessman, Alfred Cowles, who was concerned about the inability of economists to forecast what was happening in the stock market and wanted to encourage the development of improved economic techniques (he also supported the Econometric Society). The most important phase in the work of the Cowles Commission was from 1943 to 1948, under the research directorship of Jacob Marshak.

The Cowles Commission reflected not only American traditions in mathematical economics but also the ideas of a large number of European émigrés. In the 1920s many economists had been forced to leave Russia and Eastern Europe, and in the 1930s and early 1940s they were followed by those who had been forced out of Germany and Western Europe by the Nazis. Particularly important émigrés included John von Neumann (better known for his work on the atomic bomb and for designing the architecture of the modern computer); Abraham Wald, a statistician and an influential economic theorist; and Marshak himself. Marshak's career perfectly illustrates the turmoil of this period. Born in 1898 to a Jewish family in the Ukraine, he experienced the Soviet revolution of 1917 and went to study in Germany, where he embarked on an academic career in economics. In 1933 he was forced to leave Germany for England, where he spent five years at Oxford. In 1938 he went to the United States, intending to stay a year, but when war broke out he remained in the country, becoming the key figure in the Cowles Commission at its most creative period.

Under Marshak, there emerged a distinctive 'Cowles Commission approach' to economics that was highly influential in post-war economics. It emphasized the general-equilibrium characteristic of economic systems – that everything depended on everything else, which meant that to understand an economic system it was necessary to model all markets simultaneously. For example, demand conditions in the market for steel might depend on demand for canned food, the demand for which might depend on the availability of fresh food, which in turn might be affected by agricultural land being used for house building. It was assumed that markets for goods, labour and capital were perfectly competitive – that no individual trader, whether a firm or a household, could influence the market price – an assumption that was essential to make the model manageable. Economics was, therefore, dominated by the construction of models of general competitive equilibrium, often referred to simply as general-equilibrium models and the development of statistical methods that were appropriate fitting such models to economic data.

It is worth noting that the assumption that all markets were perfectly competitive was an intentionally gross simplification. In the real world, competition was often less than perfect: some markets were dominated by a single seller that could dictate prices (monopoly); in others there were small numbers of sellers, whose actions could influence prices and who had to take account of what other traders were doing. In a perfectly competitive world, there would be no room for advertising. The simplification of perfect competition was needed in order to analyse a whole economy at the same time; otherwise, the problem would become hopelessly complicated. The resulting models were thus highly abstract, and though they came to dominate the discipline, at least until the 1960s, this made them open to criticism. They illustrate perfectly that the requirement that theories be mathematically rigorous meant that economists had to deal with increasingly abstract models.

The main figures behind the statistical methods developed at Cowles in the 1940s were Tjalling Koopmans, a Dutch economist originally trained in mathematics and statistics and Trygve Haavelmo, a Norwegian who was working for the Norwegian government in New York and Washington during the war. Koopmans, in the Netherlands, had written a thesis on the problem of using regression analysis (a statistical technique for calculating the relationship between two or more variables) when there were errors in the variables, that is, when the variables were not measured accurately. Crucially, Haavelmo showed how such systems could be analysed within a formal (mathematical) probability framework. This opened up the prospect that the testing of economic theories could become much more rigorous: economists could use seemingly objective statistics methods to decide which theories best fitted the available evidence. Koopmans was also involved in another strand of the Cowles approach, the formal analysis of decision making. Before the war, he had investigated freight rates for shipping, and during the war he extended this work whilst working at the Combined Shipping Adjustment Board, to the problem of optimal use of Allied shipping.

ARROW, SAMUELSON AND FRIEDMAN

Economists might agree on the need for economics to be scientific, and they might even agree that it should be based on a theory in which individuals choose as best they can among the alternatives confronting them. However, this could be done in very different ways. The most formal approach is best represented by Kenneth Arrow and Gerard Debreu. Arrow, who spent most of his career at Stanford University in California, was trained at Columbia University, where one of his teachers was Abraham Wald, a Rumanian who in the 1930s had participated in a seminar in Vienna run by the mathematician Karl Menger. Rigorous mathematics, emphasizing the derivation of theories from a precisely specified list of assumptions (or axioms) was very much in the air. Another member of the seminar was John von Neumann, who had been responsible for working out a rigorous, axiomatic foundation for quantum mechanics in the 1920s. Wald had produced, in 1936, the first proof of the existence of general equilibrium. Note that an existence proof does not prove that equilibrium exists in the real world: it just proves that a set of equations must have a solution. Wald had explained to Arrow that the problem was very difficult, deterring him from tackling it for several years. Debreu had been trained in France as a mathematician and had been associated with the highly formalist Bourbaki group. Both became researchers at the Cowles Commission, Arrow in 1947 and Debreu in 1950. In the early 1950s they worked together on what became considered the definitive proof of the existence of general competitive equilibrium (1954). They also proved what came to be known as the two fundamental theorems of welfare economics – propositions about the efficiency of a competitive equilibrium.

Arrow's approach to economics is even more clearly illustrated in *Social Choice and Individual Values* (1951). Starting from the assumption that we know the preferences of every member of a group and a set of five ethical criteria (including that if everyone favours a particular option, it should be the group's choice and that no one should be a dictator), he asked whether there was an ethically acceptable way to derive a decision for the group as a whole. This highly abstract problem covered a wide variety of social situations. The simplest is decision making by a committee. Suppose there are three sites on which a new airport could be built and all the members of a planning committee can rank them. Arrow's problem is whether there exists a voting rule that will lead the committee to make a decision that satisfies his five ethical criteria. His conclusion was that there was not. Given that his ethical criteria seemed intuitively obvious, this was a paradoxical result. Moreover, given that the market mechanism could be considered as a mechanism for deriving a social decision (it determines who gets what), Arrow's theorem implied that the market mechanism could not be assumed to make decisions about resource allocation in an ethically acceptable way.

Another approach to constructing scientific economics was formulated by Paul Samuelson, the dominant figure in the MIT economics department after he moved there from Harvard in 1940. His approach to economics had been laid out in *Foundations of Economic Analysis* (1947), originally his Harvard doctoral dissertation. His objective is indicated by the dissertation's subtitle, 'The operational significance of economic theory'. For Samuelson, being scientific meant deriving operationally meaningful theorems: 'hypotheses about empirical data which could conceivably be refuted, if only under ideal conditions' (p. 4). The main source of such propositions lay in optimization because equilibrium typically involved maximizing or minimizing something. Consumers maximized utility, and firms maximized profits. Given his objective, Samuelson turned to different types of mathematics from Arrow and Debreu, but he was nonetheless adamant in advocating mathematical economics.

The laborious literary working over of essentially simple mathematical concepts such as is characteristic of much of modern economic theory is not only unrewarding from the standpoint of advancing the science, but involves as well mental gymnastics of a peculiarly depraved type. (Samuelson 1947, p. 6)

Samuelson's *Foundations* provided a virtual toolbox for economics theorists in the decades after its publication. A year after its publication, he had produced *Economics* (1948), the best-selling textbook that introduced scientific economics to the new generation of students.

Samuelson and Arrow shared the same view of consumers, firms and markets, but they developed their theories in very different ways. Samuelson, with his concern for operationally meaningful theorems, had no use for the type of existence proofs developed by Arrow. However, the difference between them should not be overstated. Both supported the mixed economy (a market economy in which government performed tasks that would not otherwise be undertaken) and developed reasons why competitive markets could not be relied upon to solve social problems. For example, Samuelson produced the classic account of the theory of 'public goods': goods that, once produced, are freely available to everyone irrespective of whether they pay for them, such as national defence and street lighting. Arrow worked out reasons markets might not provide health care efficiently, or encourage the optimal level of investment in new technology.

Milton Friedman, on the other hand, differed from Samuelson and Arrow on both the nature of scientific economics and on policy.

Friedman had been trained as a statistician, eventually obtaining his Ph.D. from Columbia in 1946, after which he moved to the University of Chicago, where he rapidly became one of the dominant influences. In a widely read essay, 'The Methodology of Positive Economics' (1953), Friedman argued,

The ultimate goal of a positive science is the development of a 'theory' or 'hypothesis' that yields valid and meaningful ... predictions about phenomena not yet observed. (p. 7).

The twist he added to this argument was that the realism of a theory's assumptions did not matter. Good, fruitful theories are ones that predict a lot on the basis of a little – they should abstract the important features of a problem, ignoring irrelevant details. Paradoxically, this means that good scientific theories *should* be unrealistic. He used this argument to defend the assumption of profit maximization against economists who believed it was important to test it, and to argue that economists should treat markets as though they were perfectly competitive.

In the 1950s and 1960s, Friedman views stood apart from the dominant approaches to economic theory represented by Samuelson and Arrow. All three agreed that theories need not be realistic, but this came out in different ways. Samuelson and Arrow were willing to both work with highly abstract models and to construct simpler models to tackle specific real world problems, but Friedman spurned highly abstract theory, confining himself to theories that were closely linked to concrete problems. He did not use advanced mathematics, preferring very simple models that could often be analysed graphically, or nothing more than verbal logical analysis. There was also a clear difference among the three in their views about policy. Though Arrow and Samuelson worked with a theory of perfect competition, and accepted that a competitive equilibrium would be efficient, they did not conclude that resource allocation should be left to the market. Samuelson's theory of public goods and Arrow's analyses of problems such as health care and innovation, clearly identified situations in which markets would fail. It was also assumed that if markets were not competitive, it might be necessary for government to regulate the industries concerned. Their theorizing was thus consistent with a belief in considerable government intervention to remedy these various examples of market failure. Friedman, in contrast, was much more supportive of free markets, and critical of the case for government intervention. With his University of Chicago colleague George Stigler, he was critical of unions and of attempts to regulate industry so as to ensure competition. Markets might not be perfectly competitive, but they were sufficiently competitive that they would work reasonably efficiently. Freidman and Stigler's view eventually became the dominant strand in Chicago economics.

EXPANDING THE SCOPE OF ECONOMIC THEORY

By the 1960s, mathematical theorizing had become securely established in economics. However, much economics was still conducted in a more traditional way, with verbal reasoning playing a significant role. There were two reasons for this. The first is that, although economists were by then routinely being trained in mathematics and statistics, many in the older generation did not have these skills. More importantly, however, there were still many problems that lay beyond the scope of formal modelling. The dominant theory was general competitive equilibrium, and there was great optimism that it would provide the framework into which the whole of economics would eventually be fitted. Mark Blaug has written of this period,

[T]he discipline of economics was never so confident as it was in the late 1950s and early 1960s: we *knew* that general equilibrium theory was the last word in theoretical elegance, that input–output analysis and linear programming would soon make it not just elegant but operational, and that 'the neo-classical synthesis' had successfully joined Keynesian macroeconomics [see Chapter 7 of this book] to Walrasian [general equilibrium] microeconomics; in short, that true economics was one church and that the full truth was at any moment to be revealed to us. (Backhouse and Middleton 2000, p. 207)

Yet, for all this optimism, economic theory was still very limited. There was no satisfactory theory of strategic behaviour, where one agent had to take into account how another agent would respond to his or her behaviour, and economic models assumed that consumers and firms were fully informed about the choices they were making. Koopmans, in an influential essay on methodology, had defended unrealistic economic models by arguing that they would eventually become more realistic:

[We should] look upon economic theory as a sequence of conceptional *models* that seek to express in simplified form different aspects of an always more complicated reality. ... The study of the simpler models is protected from the reproach of unreality by the consideration that these models may be prototypes of more realistic, but also more complicated, subsequent models. (Koopmans 1957, pp. 142–3)

Critics, on the other hand, doubted that the simplifying assumptions underlying these models would ever be removed.

During the 1960s and 1970s, there were several important developments in economic theory. One is that economists began to take game theory much more seriously. The theory of games was another product of interwar Vienna, and it had been applied to economics by von Neumann and another Austrian economist, Oskar Morgenstern in *The Theory of Games and Economic Behavior* (1944). It had also been the subject of some short papers by the Princeton mathematician John Nash in 1950–1, and was then worked on extensively at the RAND Corporation, a think tank set up by the U.S. Air Force (discussed in more detail in Chapter 8), where it provided a framework for analysing strategies for conducting thermonuclear war. But game theory was not applied systematically to economics until the 1960s and 1970s, when it was taken up, first in industrial economics and then in other fields, from international trade to macroeconomics. Its attraction for economists was that it provided a way to think rigorously about problems of strategy, where each player has to take account of how the other players will respond to his or her moves. It was, for example, seemingly an ideal technique with which to tackle the problem of oligopoly (competition between a small number of firms, each of which must take into account how other firms will react to anything it does), a problem to which they had no good solution.

Another change concerned information, work on which proliferated in the 1960s and 1970s. Up to this point, theories about individuals and markets had generally assumed that households and firms had full information about the environment in which their choices were being made; problems that arise from information being incomplete or asymmetric (one person knowing more than another) were either ignored or assumed away. But in the early 1960s, Stigler explored the problem of how long the rational consumer should spend searching for a low price, given that they did not know the prices charged by different stores. Arrow tackled problems arising from uncertainty and lack of information in the provision of health care. George Akerlof, from MIT, showed that if sellers knew more than buyers about the quality of the goods they were selling (his example was used cars, hence the title of his 1970 paper, "The Market for Lemons"), it may be impossible to find a price at which trade can take place. This was an example of the problem known as asymmetric information. Another MIT student, Joseph Stiglitz, along with a series of co-authors, used arguments based on imperfect information to show that asymmetric information might cause markets not to behave like the competitive supply-and-demand model suggests. For example, if banks cannot tell how risky their borrowers are, they may choose to set a low interest rate and ration credit, rather than charge a higher interest. Michael Spence, trained at Harvard, developed a theory of signalling: workers may choose education even if it does not increase their skills at all, purely to signal to employers that they have higher than average ability. This theory of signalling proved applicable to many other contexts, such as that of firms using dividends (expensive because of their tax implications) to signal that they are profitable.

These changes meant that economists were applying formal, mathematical modelling to an increasingly wide range of economic problems. Development economics is a good example. There were attempts to apply formal models to the problem of planning, but development economics remained dominated by comparatively informal theorizing. It was generally assumed that markets did not work properly and that people were not rational. There were heated debates over whether it was best for underdeveloped countries, as they were then known, to industrialize so that they had to import fewer goods or to specialize in exporting agricultural products. In the 1970s this thinking changed, as the new theories enabled economists to construct formal models. Stiglitz, for example, was able to show that share-cropping (where the tenant pays the landlord an agreed fraction of the harvest) might be preferred to money rents because it reduced the risk faced by tenants.

The scope of economic theory also expanded in that techniques developed to explain economic problems were applied to problems outside the traditional domain of the subject. A key figure here was Gary Becker, who in the 1950s applied standard economic techniques to problems at the margin of the discipline, such as discrimination and education. Education, for example, was modelled in a manner that paralleled a company's decision to invest in machinery, as the accumulation by the worker of 'human capital'. By the 1960s he had turned to problems traditionally considered to lie in the domain of sociology, such as marriage, divorce and crime. At Chicago, he ended up holding a joint appointment in economics and sociology. Around 1960, several economists (Mancur Olson, Gordon Tullock, James Buchanan and Anthony Downs) turned to problems of non-market decision making, a term that encompassed not only the analysis of social problems, but also the political process (elections, campaigning, lobbying) and the behaviour of bureaucracies, whether in government or the private sector. As with Becker's work, economists were initially sceptical about whether "public choice", as the study of behaviour within the public sector came to be known, should be considered as economics, but it eventually became an integral part of the discipline. Its significance for economic policy was that, alongside market failure caused by problems such as public goods, imperfect competition or limited information, it was necessary to take account of government failure caused by the fact that politicians and bureaucrats were themselves economic agents, concerned with their own welfare.

This period also saw dramatic changes in econometrics – the development and use of formal statistical methods for analysing economic data. Though the foundations for formal econometric methods had been laid by the 1940s, many techniques having been developed, especially at the Cowles Commission, statistical work was held back by the cost of computing. In the 1940s, electronic computers were not available to economists. It was not until the 1970s that powerful computers had become available to most universities, and the spread of personal computers did not begin till the 1980s. These advances in computer technology made possible a rapid growth in econometrics, now understood not as the integration of economic theory and statistical methods, but as a term describing the statistical, data processing techniques that were needed to handle economic data.

'ECONOMIC SCIENCE' IN THE 1990S AND BEYOND

These changes in economics, many of which dated from the 1960s and 1970s and were consolidated during the 1980s, led to economics becoming both narrower and broader. It was broader in that the range of problems tacked by means of formal theory expanded beyond anything that was possible in the 1950s. Yet at the same time, economics became narrower in that it was increasingly based on the assumption of rational, maximizing behaviour, and formal techniques, whether mathematical theory or formal statistical data analysis, were becoming the norm. Articles in the top journals were increasingly mathematical, competence in the use of mathematical modelling techniques was taken to be an indicator of proficiency as an academic economist.

This may explain the increasing attraction of the Robbins definition and why economists were more than ever willing to equate economics with the science of choice. In the 1930s and 1940s, it was seen as a problem that the Robbins definition was sufficiently broad to include subject matter belonging to the other social sciences – Becker argued that Robbins did not wish to confront the full implications of his own definition. Yet with the application of rational-choice methods in political science and sociology, and with economists from Becker to Tullock exploring social and political problems, the comprehensiveness of the Robbins definition was an advantage.

Yet, if we look beyond economic theory, we find that the Robbinsian conception of economic science did not fit what was going on in economics. Economics was becoming much more than the working out of the implications of choice under scarcity. Econometrics was offering techniques of data analysis that made it possible both to test theories and to discover empirical generalizations in ways that Robbins had not anticipated – indeed, in ways that ran against many of the assumptions he made about the economic world. The assumption that empirical generalizations were so weak that it was necessary to base economic theory on simple, self-evident assumptions (even if that were possible) could be questioned, for techniques were being developed that made it possible to derive generalizations that were much more robust than ones that had been available even twenty years earlier. In addition the new theories, from game theory to the economics of information, increasingly failed to give clear indications of how economic systems must behave: all they did was identify causal mechanisms that *could* be operating in the real world. Whether they *were* operating was an empirical question.

Economists began to believe that experimental methods might have a role to play in the subject. Experiments had been conducted as early as the 1930s, but until the 1970s there was a widely shared view that economics was not an experimental science. This changed in the 1970s and 1980s when the use of experiments spread rapidly. Laboratory experiments involve recruiting volunteers (who were often students because they were easy to recruit and willing to participate even if the cash rewards were low) to perform tasks in a controlled environment, receiving rewards that corresponded to their performance. Because they were receiving rewards (cash) that they could take out of the laboratory, experimentalists argued that they were performing real experiments, that their results could be checked, like experiments in natural science, and used to predict how people would behave outside the laboratory. Attitudes towards risk could be discovered by asking subjects to choose between a series of lotteries. Choices between lotteries could be used to test the assumptions made in economic theory. To give an example that was widely discussed in the 1970s and 1980s, when confronted with a choice between two lotteries, people should choose the one to which they attach the highest cash value, but psychologists Sarah Lichtenstein and Paul Slovic (1971) were able to construct experiments in which a substantial proportion of their subjects did not do this. Faced with this challenge to an assumption fundamental to much economic theory, this provoked responses from economists who sought both to establish whether Lichtenstein and Slovic's results were valid, and to establish whether or not they had any implications for economics.

Experimental economics was not confined to the study of how individuals made choices. There have been market experiments. Theories of competitive markets make powerful predictions about equilibrium (in which supply equals demand) but say very little about how that equilibrium is achieved – there are so many things that can happen out of equilibrium that generalization is difficult. But experiments can be constructed in which groups of subjects behave as if they were in a competitive market, and the experimenter can observe whether the price of what is being traded converges to the equilibrium predicted by economic theory, and if so, how quickly it does so. Experiments can also study how people behave when they bargain with each other, and studies of behaviour under such circumstances can be used to help design institutions (such as the best way to design an auction, as discussed in Chapter 2). It is possible to find out whether individuals are self-interested or are driven by considerations such as fairness. Take the so-called 'ultimatum game': the subject A is given $10 and is told to offer subject B a share – if B accepts the offer, they both get the agreed sums, but if B rejects it they get nothing. Rationality says that B should accept whatever is offered, because it is better than nothing, and that it is therefore in A's interest to offer very little (perhaps $1) so as to keep as much as possible. But if people are motivated by fairness, offers would be made and accepted only if close to $5. This leads into what is perhaps the most controversial, and significant application of experiments – the study of individual behaviour, testing and exploring alternatives to rationality. It was controversial because experimental work found systematic departures from rationality: in the ultimatum game many people *do* offer sums close to $5, and they reject offers that are significantly less than this, suggesting that people are motivated by notions of fairness, something that does not appear in standard theory. The increased importance of this work is illustrated by the establishment in 1986 of the Economic Science Association, concerned with 'Using controlled experiments to learn about economic behavior' (www. economicscience.org) and the award of the 2002 Nobel Memorial Prize in Economic Science to psychologist and decision theorist, Daniel Kahneman, and economist Vernon Smith.

Even more recent than experimental economics is 'behavioural economics', a name for approaches to economics that draws on insights from psychology. Behavioural economics may involve the use of experiments but need not do so. Information from experiments may be combined with, for example, information from systematic observation of how people behave in real world situations. 'Herding', for example, is the phenomenon that people are often influenced by the behaviour of people around them. This can be tested in the laboratory, or by observing groups of consumers, investors or even judges making decisions in court. It has been particularly important in finance, where, in the eyes of many economists, it is the only thing that can explain asset price 'bubbles', where the prices of assets such as stocks or housing rise far above what the underlying economic conditions suggest they are worth. Another approach involves the use of happiness surveys, where people are asked questions such as 'Taking all things together, are you very happy, quite happy or not very happy?', or are asked a series of questions such as 'Have you felt depressed recently?', 'Are you satisfied with your life?', which are then coded into an overall score. There is clearly a significant degree of arbitrariness in how any individual will answer such questions, but it has been found that there are clear patterns in the responses when large samples of people are used. This is a technique developed by psychologists, taken over by economists. Even more clearly linked with psychology is 'Neuroeconomics', using devices such as MRI scanners to measure the brain activity taking place whilst subjects are taking economic decisions. Some economists have used experiments to support traditional positions, but the real significance of these developments is that they hold out a way to undertake rigorous, scientific economics without relying on the assumption that individuals are rational.

The lesson from this chapter is that many of the developments in thinking about microeconomics during the period since the Second World War need to be understood as the result of economists trying to be scientific. The increased abstraction of economic theory compared with what was normal in the 1930s, or compared with what non-economists can understand, is the result of attempting to be rigorous: without making simplifying assumptions, it would have been impossible to show that economists' conclusions did indeed follow from the assumptions that they were making. This came to be tied up with a changed conception of what economics was. For around two decades, the focus was on general competitive equilibrium as the most rigorous form of economic theory, but from the 1960s and 1970s economists began to develop models that could not be seen as simplifications of this theory: game theory and models of limited information were radically different. However, they remained abstract, though in a different way: theories were of necessity tailored to specific situations and made no claim to be presenting a theory of how the economy must operate. Statements about the real world were the province of applied economists who, though they might use economic theory, used econometric (statistical) techniques to test and apply it using an ever-increasing range of data, from the national accounts to surveys of thousands of individual households and workers. Towards the end of the century, the rhetoric of being scientific was taken up again by advocates of experimental and behavioural economics, this time emphasizing the use of techniques that could be used to find out how people actually behaved. These developments form the background to what happened in macroeconomics during the same period, though there the interaction between theory and empirical practices was different.

The Quest for Rigorous Macroeconomics

How did economics come to be dominated by theories that, in the opinion of a significant number of economists, either led to serious policy errors, or, at best, distracted economists from the issues that needed to be addressed? This chapter leaves aside the possible role played by ideology (discussed in Chapter 8) and explores the extent to which the desire to develop a rigorous, 'scientific' macroeconomics was a major factor behind the subject evolving in the way that it did.

The turning point in twentieth-century discussions of what is now called 'macroeconomics', or the study of economy as a whole, including the problems of money, inflation, unemployment, economic growth and the business cycle, was undoubtedly the publication of *The General Theory of Employment, Interest and Money* (1936) by the Cambridge economist, John Maynard Keynes. Keynes did not invent macroeconomics – theorizing on such topics has a very long history, and neither did Keynes invent the term – but the *General Theory* was the main route through which ideas developed in the interwar period entered modern economics. His book provided the framework on which macroeconomics was rapidly reconstructed during and after the 1940s.

The need to reconstruct the subject grew in part out of the move towards formal modelling. The *General Theory* provided a set of components out of which economists could construct formal, mathematical models that could be used to analyse the effects of policy changes on variables such as the level of economic activity and the unemployment rate. Economists were, as was explained in Chapter 6, becoming 'model builders', and Keynes provided the raw materials. National accounts, which had been started before the war, were reorganized during the Second World War using categories (such as national income, consumption, investment) that corresponded with the definitions in *General Theory*. During the war, Keynesian theory, in conjunction with data from the national accounts, was used in planning, both to control inflation and to work out how much productive capacity was available for the war effort.

However, though the *General Theory* was taken up by economists concerned with constructing mathematical models, Keynes himself did not think in this way. He had been trained in mathematics, and his argument reflected a mathematician's way of thinking – it was full of the language of functions, schedules and propensities. Yet, much of the book was devoted to the analysis of concepts and to reasoning that was based on his direct observation of the world around him (he had considerable experience in the City of London and was an accomplished speculator and financial adviser) and on his intuitions about how the world worked. Furthermore, many of the key arguments in the book were made using verbal reasoning, not figuring in the formal mathematical apparatus around which the book was constructed. The result was that though economists were inspired by the book, finding many valuable ideas in it, and although it did contain the elements around which a mathematical model could be built, many of his arguments appeared 'unscientific' by the standards economists were increasingly applying. This was something economists rapidly sought to put right.

Keynes's main idea was that the level of economic activity in the economy, which might be measured by national income or the level of employment, was determined by aggregate demand for goods and services. This meant that if aggregate demand were too low, production and income would be low, and unemployment would be high. It was of course possible that demand would be sufficiently high that there would be full employment, and if that were the case, rises in demand would produce inflation. However, he argued that there were no automatic mechanisms that would guarantee full employment. In particular, cutting wages would not raise employment because there could be no assurance that this would raise the level of aggregate demand. Indeed, if wage cuts reduced workers' spending or caused people to be pessimistic about the future, they might even create more unemployment. The argument that high wages priced workers out of jobs might work for the individual worker, but it did not work at the level of the economy as a whole. Similarly, increased saving would make the situation worse, not better, because it would reduce the level of spending and cut aggregate demand. The remedy for unemployment was, Keynes argued, to raise investment, either through monetary policy, that is, by lowering interest rates so that firms invested more, or through direct state action to raise investment. This would raise employment and, because this would raise consumption, income would rise by even more than investment. If, for example, consumers spent three-quarters of their income on consumption, each dollar spent on investment would raise incomes by a dollar, which would raise consumption spending by 75 cents. That 75 cents of spending would raise income by 75 cents, causing consumption to rise by a further 56 cents (three-quarters of 75 cents) and so on. Adding up this sequence of increases in income, Keynes showed that, in this example, each dollar of extra investment would cause income to rise by $4 (this was the multiplier).

Economists sought to make Keynesian macroeconomics more rigorous in four ways. The first is that the equations Keynes proposed in *General Theory* were put together into a complete model, from which economists sought to prove, using algebra or geometry, that all his conclusions were correct. This was based on the so-called 'circular flow of income' according to which everyone's spending was someone else's income. Equilibrium in this flow of income required that, when the different sectors of the economy are considered as a whole, planned spending must equal what is being received as income. Thus, if households are spending less than they receive as income (if they are saving part of their income) equilibrium requires that another sector (firms or the government) is spending more than it is receiving as income. Models of this process came in several sizes. The simplest had one equation and showed little more than how the multiplier worked. Yet, it still suggested important conclusions, such as that cutting government spending, though it might reduce the government deficit, would typically cause unemployment to rise. Or the model could be expanded with a model of the money market, so that two equations explained both the level of output and the rate of interest – the so-called IS-LM model, named after the labels used for its two equations. This showed that interest rate rises might, under certain circumstances, choke off rises in output, causing the multiplier to be lower than it would otherwise be. It also showed how raising the money supply could cause expansion by lowering the rate of interest, unless the rate of interest hit a floor, below which it could not go – the so-called liquidity trap. Or the model could be complicated further, so that other factors that were 'off-stage' in the simple models, were modelled explicitly. This might include adding an equation to describe the behaviour of the labour market (how are wages affected by unemployment, and how does this affect other variables in the model?) or it might involve modelling the financial sector in more detail (allowing for a range of financial assets and hence more than one rate of interest).

However, although these models were simple, they were also static and remained purely theoretical. This meant that they could be made more realistic either by modelling the way variables changed over time or by estimating the sizes of different coefficients from real-world data. Once economists moved beyond very simple models, these two features went together, for two reasons. The first is that dynamic modelling of more than one or two variables gets complicated, and it typically becomes very hard to say what will happen using theory alone. The theorist needs to know how big some of the numbers in the model are to be able to work out how it will behave. The second is that when equations are estimated using real-world data, the result is typically a dynamic model. For example, consumption expenditure does not depend only on households' current income: it will depend on their wealth (on past saving) and on expectations concerning the future. It is, using the economist's jargon, an 'inter-temporal' decision: because saving enables households to consume more income in the future, it involves choices over time. Similarly, investment (about purchasing capital goods that will produce output over a period of time) and transactions in financial assets are also based on inter-temporal decisions.

These three developments: (1) mathematical modelling, plus (2) taking account of dynamics, and (3) incorporating real-world data into the models culminated in the creation of large macroeconomic models that were used by governments and central banks to forecast the economy. By the 1960s and early 1970s, such models had become very large, some having as many as 2,000 equations, so as to depict the economy in great detail. They required not only immense computing power (at least by the standards of the time) and large teams of economists, each working on a different part of the model: one group might focus entirely on modelling demand for durable consumption goods, whilst another might simply model the behaviour of wages. However, though these models became complicated, they remained developments of the basic Keynesian theory, according to which the level of aggregate demand determined the level of output.

THE SEARCH FOR MICRO-FOUNDATIONS

There was, however, a fourth way in which economists sought to make macroeconomic theories more rigorous, and it proved decisive in dictating the route followed by macroeconomics in the 1970s and after. It was what, around the 1970s, came to be called the search for 'micro-foundations' for macroeconomic theory.

As was explained earlier, Keynes had built his theory by reasoning on the basis of his direct observations of the world around him. It was, he argued, 'a fundamental psychological law' that as someone's income rose, they would increase their consumption but devote a smaller fraction of their income to consumption while saving a larger fraction. This view accords with common sense and with statistical data because the poorest households have no choice but to spend all their income, whilst the rich can save large amounts (further increasing their wealth). Similarly, Keynes's analysis of financial markets was based on observations such as that, when faced with the need to make decisions about an uncertain future, people are guided by what they see others doing, and they assume that the future will generally be substantially like the present. For the economists who came after him, the main problem with these arguments was not that they were incorrect: it was that they were not rigorous. Macroeconomic relationships are the outcome of decisions by millions of individuals, which means that if the subject is to be rigorous, it must be based on a theory of how individuals behave.

As Chapter 6 has shown, the dominant theory in the period since the Second World War has been that individuals are rational, maximizing agents. Combine this with the notion of rigour discussed in Chapter 6, and the conclusion is that the macroeconomic theorist should start with the assumption that individuals are rational, and then show how actions by individuals, when aggregated (when the actions of millions of individuals are put together) produce the relationships that are used in macroeconomic theories. Unlike in Keynes's *General Theory*, these theories about individuals should take the form of mathematical models, and aggregation should be rigorous. In that way, starting from axioms about individual rationality and precisely stated assumptions about the constraints facing them (what information do they have and how do markets work?) it is possible to derive a theory in which predictions about, say, how a rise in government spending will influence unemployment, can be derived completely rigorously.

Of course, such theories would need to be tested against real-world data. But the belief was that, because the assumptions being made about individuals and markets were basically correct, rigorously derived theories would be more successful than less rigorous ones. Econometric work, analysing statistical data, routinely showed that simple theories failed to account for everything that was going on, sometimes falling down badly, and that the answer was better theories. But there was also the problem that empirical work did not appear to be capable of providing answers on its own: there were simply too many models that could be fitted to the data, meaning that theory was essential. More than this, in a real sense, economists had more confidence in theory than in data. Theories based on rational behaviour and competitive markets seemed to work well when explaining what went on in individual markets, and given their intuitive appeal, the burden of proof was on those who denied them. On the other side, econometrics had progressed greatly since even the 1940s, but its methods were still very limited, and it was very hard to derive robust empirical relationships. For example, if a study found that a one percentage point rise in unemployment would cause wage inflation to be two percentage points higher than it would otherwise have been, economists could not be confident that this number would not change significantly the following year.

In the late 1940s and 1950s, economists developed rigorous theories in which macroeconomic models were derived from general equilibrium foundations, represented by *Money, Interest and Prices* (1956), by the Chicago-trained economist and one-time member of the Cowles Commission, Don Patinkin. His starting point was a rigorous theory of household behaviour, from which he derived formal macroeconomic models such as were being widely used. Patinkin thereby offered a framework that could be used to tackle many of the theoretical issues surrounding Keynesian economics. However, in many ways, the model remained static: it focussed on what determined equilibrium output at any moment, but did not tackle issues such as the business cycle, inflation or the formation of expectations and their impact on the economy. These were all to become important problems in the 1970s. In addition, though macroeconomic theory might be rigorous, there remained a significant gap between theory and practice as represented by the large-scale forecasting models. Those models, as explained above, were large and arguably ramshackle constructions: individual components might have rigorous micro-foundations, and the overall framework was consistent with theory, but they were simply too large and complicated to be integrated wholes.

During the 1960s, economic theorists raised a number of questions about this approach. In 1959, Kenneth Arrow pointed to a number of conceptual problems with the general equilibrium framework on which the drive towards micro-foundations rested: out of equilibrium, where supply and demand did not balance, it was logically impossible that everyone could sell as much as they wanted at the prevailing market price, which meant that competition could not be perfect. Robert Clower argued that to understand Keynesian theory it was necessary to take account of the fact that if members of a household could not work as much as they wanted, they would have to cut back on their consumption. This provided a reason that 'disequilibrium' (supply not equal to demand) in one market would have repercussions, which were not allowed for in models of general competitive equilibrium, on other markets, that is, spillover effects. Of course, if there were some mechanism to ensure that all markets were in equilibrium, Arrow's and Clower's concerns would not matter, but, as Axel Leijonhufvud argued in a highly influential book, *On Keynesian Economics and the Economics of Keynes* (1968), there was no such device: the world did not have a master auctioneer who would, as a *deus ex machina*, ensure that everyone's activity harmonized with everyone else's.

The problems identified by Arrow and Clower were a fact of life. Moreover, the existence of unemployment was taken as evidence that there must be disequilibrium, at least in the labour market. And this was not all, for there was also a substantial literature arguing that, in a world where there was enormous diversity amongst households and firms, rigorous aggregation was impossible. What this meant was that, in general, the behaviour of a heterogeneous group of individuals (whether firms or households) would not necessarily resemble the behaviour of any of the individuals. In the late 1960s and early 1970s these and other developments resulted in an explosion of literature that tried to establish more rigorous micro-foundations for Keynesian economics.

MONETARISM AND THE CRISIS OF THE 1970S

For almost three decades after the Second World War, Keynesianism was dominant, its dominance in economic theory chiming with its importance as a plank of the social philosophy that formed the basis for the welfare state. There might be problems with the theory, but so long as Western economies were broadly successful – and, after all, even if they had made mistakes, policy makers had managed to avoid a repeat of the disasters that befell the world economy during the 1930s – there was no reason to question it. However, not all economists accepted this consensus, and one of these was the Chicago economist, Milton Friedman.

To understand Friedman's approach to economics, it is necessary to remember that much of his early career was spent at the NBER. The NBER represented the older conception of scientific rigor, discussed in Chapter 6, according to which scientific rigour meant not logical rigour but meticulously grounding science on empirical foundations. The focus of the NBER was on generating statistics on income, consumption, wealth and a myriad of other variables; NBER economists, Simon Kuznets and Robert Nathan, were key figures in the development of the U.S. national accounts in the 1930s and 1940s. The economist whose vision inspired the NBER approach, Wesley Clair Mitchell, saw his work on the business cycle, not as testing a specific theory, but as providing a detailed statistical description of what happened in business cycles that would establish the timing of various aspects of the cycle and the relative importance of the various factors that might cause it. Statistics were combined with 'business annals' based on contemporary opinions about business conditions. Thus although Mitchell's work was informed by economic theory, he never saw the need to make it mathematically rigorous, for rigour meant taking the evidence seriously and providing a thorough, objective account of what was going on in the world.

This attitude towards economic theory placed the NBER in opposition to the Cowles Commission (see Chapter 6). Whereas Cowles stood for rigour as the term was coming to be understood in science, the NBER stood for the older tradition. This difference erupted in an exchange that took place in 1947, occasioned by Koopman's review of the latest NBER opus on business cycles, *Measuring Business Cycles*, (Burns and Mitchell 1945). The controversy is worth discussing briefly, because it goes to the heart of many modern arguments about how economics should be conducted.

Koopmans argued that the work of Burns and Mitchell represented what he called the 'Kepler stage' in economics (Johannes Kepler, the German mathematician and astronomer, had described the elliptical motion of the planets round the sun), whereas what was needed was to move towards the 'Newton stage', in which observation was structured by theory. For example, Burns and Mitchell measured business cycles using observations of seven variables, ranging from pig-iron production and orders for railroad freight cars to the number of shares traded and the volume of bank clearings. But without a model, it was impossible to know whether these were the relevant variables to choose. The NBER approach, Koopmans contended, was 'measurement without theory'.

In his response for the NBER, Rutledge Vining objected that the Cowles Commission were asking economists to take their methods on trust, for there was no evidence that economic models of the type advocated by Koopmans were any more reliable in their predictions than less formal approaches. Until they were found to conform to stable relationships in the data, the notion of an 'underlying behaviour equation', on which the Cowles approach relied, was 'utterly devoid of content' (Hendry and Morgan 1995, p. 522). Vining also argued that the NBER methods were about 'discovery and hypothesis-seeking': if one knew what the correct theory was (as Cowles claimed they did), this might not matter, but the correct theory was not known. He questioned the very idea that economics must be based on theories about individual behaviour, arguing that aggregates need not behave like the individuals of which they were made up. One can, for example, understand how a colony of ants behaves without having any theory about how any individual ant behaves.

When, in 1948, Friedman and Anna Schwartz, embarked on their project on money and the business cycle, their methods were those of the NBER. Friedman presented this work in 'The Quantity Theory of Money: a Restatement' (1956) as having a theory that was very different from that of the prevailing Keynesian orthodoxy. The key variable, he argued, was the quantity of money. However, rather than adopt the conventional strategy of developing a formal theoretical model with which he could prove that money mattered, he resorted to empirical work. He, Schwartz and a number of other colleagues trawled systematically through statistical data searching for evidence that supported their claims that demand for money was a stable function of income and a few other variables such as interest rates, and that money had powerful effects on the economy, though the lags involved were long and variable (the effects of a monetary stimulus or contraction would not be felt for at least eighteen months, and it might take three years). His more orthodox colleagues, such as James Tobin, were frustrated by his way of arguing, because he failed to show them a theory that was any different from that used by Keynesians, and because they believed that his correlations did not say anything about causation: the crucial issue was not whether money was strongly correlated with prices or income, but whether monetary changes caused changes in the economy, or the other way round.

Friedman and Schwartz's answer to this challenge appeared in their book, *A Monetary History of the United States, 1861–1960* (1963). This book used the quantity theory of money to tell the story of the relationship between money, output and prices in the United States over the previous century. Perhaps their most significant argument was that the Great Depression of 1929–32 had occurred, not because monetary policy could do nothing, but because the Federal Reserve had taken a disastrous series of decisions, allowing the money supply to fall catastrophically. Though economists and historians might question this account, it provided a clear and very powerful alternative to the Keynesian view that slumps originated in the private sector, and that key to the Depression was a collapse in investment.

It was out of such arguments that Friedman and other economists who believed there were problems with the Keynesian orthodoxy began to formulate the ideas that came to be known by the term 'monetarism'. Because of what happened later, it is important to be clear about what this doctrine meant in the hands of Friedman and his contemporaries. The first point is that monetarism was the doctrine that there was, over long periods of time, a connection between changes in the money supply and inflation. There might be no clear relationship between them over short periods of time, during which monetary expansion might lead to rises in output and falls in unemployment, but if monetary expansion was high for several years, this would eventually be followed in a period of high inflation. This result was, they believed, borne out by a weight of statistical evidence, for many countries and over many decades.

Monetarist policy conclusions followed from this, namely, that policy should be aimed at achieving a stable growth rate of the money supply. Such a rule would have prevented the Great Depression because if the money supply had not been allowed to collapse, there would have been no catastrophe. Similarly, such a rule would have prevented the policies that had caused major inflations, with their disruptive consequences. In theory, it might be possible to do better than what could be achieved by a monetary growth rule, but the long and variable lags identified by Friedman and his colleagues meant that it would in practice be impossible to operate a stabilization policy that would improve performance. Stabilization policy was in practice more likely to destabilize the economy.

In the late 1960s and early 1970s, there were strains on the U.S. economy caused by the cost of President Johnson's War on Poverty and the simultaneous escalation of the Vietnam War at a time when the economy had already been brought to near-full employment by the successful application of Keynesian fiscal policies. As a result, the inflation rate began to rise. There was a worldwide expansion, and many countries grew rapidly in 1972–3. As demand rose, the prices of basic commodities rose. An exception to this was oil, where capacity was high. That changed in 1973 with the Yom Kippur War, after which the Arab-dominated oil exporting countries successfully formed a cartel, raising the price of oil fourfold. The expansion was brought to an abrupt halt with a collapse in world demand (the oil exporters suddenly had enormous revenues that they could not immediately spend, whilst oil importers were forced to cut back their spending to pay for oil) and inflation. In addition, technology that had been efficient when energy prices were low suddenly became uneconomic because firms could no longer afford the fuel bills, and capital needed to be modernised to be more energy efficient. For exactly the same reason, many households scrapped their gas-guzzling cars and switched to smaller, more fuel-efficient models. The collapse in demand led to unemployment and the phenomenon of 'stagflation', simultaneously rising inflation and unemployment.

Against this background, monetarism became far more persuasive. Even if people doubted Friedman's empirical work, the data generated during the 1970s dispelled doubt that money and prices were connected: in the United Kingdom, for example, the growth rate of the money supply rose from around 10 per cent in 1970 to 25 per cent in 1973, falling back to under 8 per cent in 1975. Inflation, still only 8 per cent in 1972, peaked at almost 25 per cent in 1975, falling back to around 8 cent by 1978. This appeared to clearly indicate a two-year lag. Though inflation rates were generally lower, such patterns could be found in many other countries, including the United States. Of course, there were many factors suggesting that non-monetary causes might be operating, but there had been a significant change in the weight of evidence.

At the same time, the evidence also appeared to support an argument Friedman had made very publicly in his presidential address to the American Economic Association (AEA) in 1967 and published in 1968, namely, that there was a 'natural rate' of unemployment, and if policy makers aimed for a rate above this, inflation would accelerate because rising inflation would raise expectations of inflation, causing inflation to rise still further. Unemployment was simply not a variable that the government could control, reinforcing his argument that policy should be directed at the growth rate of the money supply. A myth also developed that Keynesian economists had failed to anticipate that any attempt to create full employment would lead to stagflation. In reality, the Council of Economic Advisers (CEA), comprising economists with impeccable Keynesian credentials, had warned of the danger, but Johnson was unable to reduce U.S. commitments in Vietnam and unwilling to scale back his Great Society programme. In the words of one CEA member, Yale economist James Tobin, referring to the Keynesian economics that was applied in the United States during the 1960s,

The validity of the New Economics as a science [wa]s ... not impaired but rather reinforced by the fact that bad things happened as predicted when the advice of its practitioners was rejected. The economic efficacy of fiscal policy [wa]s confirmed, not refuted, by the powerful stimulus that Vietnam deficit spending delivered to the economy. (quoted in Bernstein 2001, p. 151)

Proposals for a tax increase to reduce the inflationary threat came to nothing because of political opposition to implementing an unpopular measure solely on the basis of a forecast: indeed, because of its clear unpopularity, few economists were willing to sign on. But Friedman and critics of the Keynesian policies pursued in the 1960s were nonetheless able to create the myth that Keynesianism had failed. Of course, once stagflation had set in, policy makers faced new problems that needed new solutions, but that is a different point.

CONTEMPORARY MACROECONOMICS

At this point, the story could be carried forward into the debates through which monetarism influenced policy during the 1970s and 1980s (that lie behind the discussions of UK monetary policy in Chapter 5). However, for the purposes of the argument being made here, it is the developments in academic economics that are more important, and the key figure is not Friedman, but Robert Lucas, a Chicago Ph.D. whose first position, from 1963 to 1974, was in the Graduate School of Industrial Administration (GSIA) at Carnegie-Mellon. The GSIA (discussed further in Chapter 8) was strongly influenced by Herbert Simon, whose career spanned economics, management science and psychology. This was important because of the focus on viewing firms and economic agents as information-processing systems, the behaviour of which could be analysed using formal mathematical techniques. Lucas became part of this community, working on problems of optimal investment and firms' production decisions.

In 1969, Edmund Phelps brought together a group of economists who were all working on the problem of how prices, wages, output and employment would behave when there was incomplete information, to produce a volume, *Microeconomic Foundations of Employment and Inflation Theory* (1970). The approach that ran through this volume directly reflected developments in microeconomics during the 1960s and inevitably focused attention on disequilibrium and dynamics. For in equilibrium, problems with information are comparatively minor. In one of the papers in the volume, published two years earlier in the *Journal of Political Economy*, Phelps had produced an argument very similar to that used by Friedman in his AEA presidential address, though it differed from Friedman's in that it was based on a formal mathematical model of behaviour under conditions of limited information, explaining phenomena such as why job vacancies could exist alongside unemployment.

Lucas was one of the contributors to this volume, writing, with Leonard Rapping, a chapter that laid out a model of the labour market that they then fitted to U.S. data. When confronted with imperfect information, the workers in these models would sometimes make mistakes and end up being unemployed. The key feature of their model was that unemployment was voluntary – the result of workers' choices. In their model, unemployed workers were 'persons who regard the wage rates at which they could currently be employed as temporarily low, and who therefore choose to wait or search for improved conditions rather than to invest in moving or changing their occupation' (Phelps 1970, p. 285). In short, a banker who had been fired but refused to take a job flipping burgers in McDonald's, was modelled as choosing to be unemployed so that he or she could try to find something better. Focusing on limited information and search models had led to new ways to conceptualize unemployment; Keynesian economists had seen unemployment as involuntary, reflecting situations where, even if the unemployed offered to work for lower wages, there would still be no jobs for them. Indeed, this was in a sense the essence of Keynesian economics: if workers could negotiate themselves into jobs by accepting wage cuts, it would be hard to say that unemployment was caused by deficient aggregate demand.

This idea, that unemployment should be modelled as voluntary, was developed into a theory in which fluctuations in output were caused purely by errors in expectations: if everyone correctly anticipated the future, markets would be in equilibrium with supply and demand, and there would be full employment. Lucas then combined this theory with the idea of 'rational expectations' to develop what came to be called the 'new classical macroeconomics'. Suppose that people used a certain rule for forecasting inflation. If that rule generates forecasts that are systematically wrong, people will realize it and modify their forecasting rule. A rational forecast is therefore one that generates expectations that differ from what is observed only through random, unpredictable errors. In 'Expectations and the Neutrality of Money' (1972), Lucas combined these different ideas to produce a model with dramatic implications. The only cause of fluctuations in unemployment, in his model, was unpredictable monetary policy because this would cause people to make mistakes, thereby generating short-term fluctuations in output and employment. This was a much stronger reason for opposing government intervention than anything Friedman and the monetarists had provided.

Lucas followed this paper with one that mounted a direct attack on Keynesian models: 'Econometric Policy Evaluation: A Critique' (1976). If economic agents are rational and take account of all the information relevant to their decisions, how is it that Keynesian models, which do not incorporate rational expectations, could have worked? Lucas's answer was that if policy follows a particular rule (maybe it has a rule linking policy to the unemployment rate) the economy will generate data that exhibits certain regularities. As long as the government policy rule does not change, these regularities can be measured and used as the basis for macroeconomic models. This, Lucas argued, is what Keynesian modellers were doing. But if the policy regime changes, behaviour will change and models based on regularities observed under the old regime will be useless. That, he argued, is why the Keynesian forecasting models had broken down after 1973. The only way to avoid this problem was to construct models based on the allegedly unchanging 'deep structural parameters' of tastes and technology.

The policy conclusions implied by Lucas's model no doubt appealed to some economists, but for many (perhaps most) economists they did not. Yet his approach to economics caught on rapidly because it offered a seemingly rigorous way to tackle the dynamic problems relating to inflation and unemployment that economists were forced to tackle in the 1970s. Rational expectations caught on not because economists believed that expectations were completely rational, but because there were demonstrable problems with any theory that postulated anything else. To assert that expectations were not rational did not go very far without some explanation of how and when departures from rationality took place.

Lucas proposed that the business cycle was driven by monetary shocks (random variations in the growth rate of the money supply), but during 1970s this was fairly quickly called into question. The hypothesis simply did not fit the data. One response was to accept the basics of Lucas's approach, including rational expectations, but to postulate that the shocks that drove the business cycle were 'real' shocks, involving random changes in the growth rate of productivity. The key proponents of this approach were Fynn Kydland and Edward Prescott, from Minnesota, who developed it into real business cycle (RBC) theory.

Another was to challenge the assumption, made by both Lucas and RBC theorists, that markets were in equilibrium with supply always equal to demand. So-called 'new Keynesian' economists developed models that accepted many of the Lucasian innovations but challenged the assumption that supply and demand for labour were always equal to each other: theories of asymmetric information (see Chapter 6), long-term contracts, and imperfect competition were used to show that, even with rational expectations, Keynesian phenomena might still emerge. In Europe, where unemployment remained stubbornly high during the 1980s, new classical and RBC theories were much less plausible than in the United States, where unemployment in the early 1980s had fallen fairly quickly.

Eventually, it became clear that the simplicities of the early RBC theories had to be abandoned and rigidities introduced. By the 1990s, this process was well underway, with the result that the distinctions between RBC and new Keynesian models became blurred. However, what came to be known as the DSGE (dynamic stochastic general equilibrium model), the model used by both New Classical and RBC theorists, remained the workhorse of macroeconomic theorizing. Its appeal stemmed from the fact that it presented a scientific way to do macroeconomics with strong micro-foundations, permitting the rigorous analysis of dynamic problems.

Scientific rigour was, however, bought at a price. Recall that in the late 1970s, economists had been raising doubts about the coherence of the general equilibrium models, yet general equilibrium models were, in this literature, the basis for what was claimed to be rigorous macroeconomic theorizing. The doubts of economists such as Arrow, Clower and Leijonhufvud about conventional theory had centred on the problems that would arise if markets were not in equilibrium. Some economists, such as France's Edmond Malinvaud, in a short and very widely cited book *The Theory of Unemployment Reconsidered* (1977), went further and contended that the 1970s stagflation demonstrated that markets were not in supply-and-demand equilibrium. In complete contrast, the new classical economists, and following them RBC theorists, simply assumed that they were: they avoided the conceptual problems that had been raised in relation to general equilibrium theory by simply assuming that supply must always equal demand. The objection that it *must* take time for human beings to take action that would bring markets into equilibrium was brushed aside. Similarly, aggregation problems were ignored by the device of the so-called representative agent. Effectively, it was assumed in the new classical and RBC models that all agents were identical, thereby eliminating aggregation problems. This is an extraordinarily strong assumption. Note that a world of identical agents is one where there are no differences between rich and poor; it also means that, because everyone has the same expectations of the future (agents are identical in *all* respects), there is no reason for trade in financial assets to take place. A world of identical agents is therefore, necessarily very different from the one in which we live.

The crucial question here is whether the fact that people are not all the same matters when looking at the economy as a whole. The strategy of

simplifying the world in order to analyse mechanisms that would otherwise remain incomprehensible is, in principle, entirely legitimate. It
can also be argued that this strategy was productive: focussing on policy
regimes and taking account of the fact that the private sector might try
to anticipate policy actions taken by government clearly focussed on
important problems that might otherwise have been neglected. However, the price was the production of models that served to foster the
view that markets worked so smoothly that government intervention
was not necessary. There remained economists who constructed models
in which markets were less than perfect, but they were on the defensive.

MACROECONOMICS AND THE CRISIS OF 2007–8

During the period of steady growth and low inflation that Federal
Reserve chairman, Ben Bernanke (2004) called 'the great moderation',
macroeconomics appeared to have put the failures of the 1970s and
1980s behind it. The move towards a consensus based on DSGE models
was accompanied by policies, centred on inflation targeting, that were
consistent with those models and appeared to have avoided the sometimes severe policy mistakes of those decades. Thus, although Bernanke
recognized that the great moderation might have been the result of structural change (such as productivity growth resulting from the application
of information technology or reducing barriers to trade) or simply been
good luck, he felt confident enough to claim that 'improved monetary
policy' had been more important in bringing it about than had generally
been recognized. This improved policy was closely linked to advances in
macroeconomic theory.

One of those who questioned this widely-held view was Paul Krugman, a Princeton trade theorist turned *New York Times* columnist, who
as early as 1999 had warned of what he called 'the return of depression
economics'. He did not claim that depression in the world economy had
returned, or even that it was likely to recur very soon, but that it had
become clear that financial-market panics could arise and that they
might lead to demand being insufficient to maintain full employment.
The world was, in his view, a much more dangerous place than talk of
a great moderation implied. After the 2007–8 financial crisis showed

that the world had, indeed, become a dangerous place, many economists concluded that macroeconomic theory had served to conceal rather than identify potential problems. To quote Krugman,

Unfortunately, this romanticized and sanitized vision of the economy led most economists to ignore all the things that can go wrong. They turned a blind eye to the limitations of human rationality that often lead to bubbles and busts; to the problems of institutions that run amok; to the imperfections of markets – especially financial markets – that can cause the economy's operating system to undergo sudden, unpredictable crashes; and to the dangers created when regulators don't believe in regulation. (*New York Times* 6 September 2009).

Because of Krugman's prominence as a newspaper columnist, which makes it easy for some critics to dismiss his work as politically motivated, it is important to stress that he is expressing a view that is echoed by respected macroeconomists without such a profile. For example, Willem Buiter, professor at the LSE and a founder member of the Bank of England's Monetary Policy Committee from 1997–2000, and whose Ph.D. had been supervised by Tobin, wrote an assessment that appeared under the heading, 'The Unfortunate Uselessness of Most 'State of the Art' Academic Monetary Economics'.

The Monetary Policy Committee ... contained ... quite a strong representation of academic economists and other professional economists with serious technical training and backgrounds. This turned out to be a severe handicap when the central bank had to switch gears and change from being an inflation-targeting central bank under conditions of orderly financial markets to a financial stability-oriented central bank under conditions of widespread market illiquidity and funding illiquidity. Indeed, the typical graduate macroeconomics and monetary economics training received at Anglo-American universities during the past 30 years or so, may have set back by decades serious investigations of aggregate economic behaviour and economic policy-relevant understanding. It was a privately and socially costly waste of time and other resources. (http://blogs.ft.com/maverecon/ p=667, 3 March 2009)

Buiter's charge is that 'state of the art' macroeconomics proved actively misleading when financial stability became an issue. Even if the theory had been useful earlier on (and he is non-committal on this) it diverted attention away from what proved to be key problems. Buiter continued by making it clear precisely which parts of macroeconomics he was criticizing.

Most mainstream macroeconomic theoretical innovations since the 1970s (the
New Classical rational expectations revolution associated with such names as
Robert E. Lucas Jr., Edward Prescott, Thomas Sargent, Robert Barro etc, and
the New Keynesian theorizing of Michael Woodford and many others) [mostly
theories based on the DSGE model] have turned out to be self-referential,
inward-looking distractions at best. Research tended to be motivated by the
internal logic, intellectual sunk capital and esthetic puzzles of established
research programmes rather than by a powerful desire to understand how the
economy works – let alone how the economy works during times of stress and
financial instability. So the economics profession was caught unprepared when
the crisis struck. (ibid.)

Buiter then listed the technical problems with these models, including
their reliance on assumptions of complete and efficient markets.

Neither Krugman nor Buiter is rejecting the use of mathematical
models in principle. Both are accomplished model-builders, a characteristic that distinguishes them sharply from many of the heterodox economists discussed in Chapter 9. Their claim is that the models dominating
macroeconomics in the past two decades have been based on inappropriate assumptions, and that this has been driven not by ideology (a
possibility explored in Chapter 8) but by the models' aesthetic appeal.
Faced with the choice between rigorous models based on questionable
assumptions and what might be termed 'messier' theories based on more
realistic assumptions, most macroeconomists have opted for the former.
Had economists remained conscious of the limitations of their models,
this choice would not have been a problem. After all, economic models
are simplifications, designed to illuminate a particular phenomenon, not
to provide a theory of everything. Nevertheless, this outcome did not
happen: the models served to deflect attention from issues that turned
out, after 2007, to be crucial.

8

Science and Ideology

FROM THE MIXED ECONOMY TO FREE-MARKETS

At the end of the Second World War, there was, outside the Soviet bloc, broad acceptance of the need for a mixed economy. There were differences over where to draw the line between the private and public sectors (for example, should basic industries be nationalized?); over the best form of economic planning, and over the appropriate level of redistribution, but the principle that the state should have a presence in economic activity was widely accepted. This had been the result of the perceived success of planning in the United States and Britain during the Second World War. Keynesian economics had established the idea that macroeconomic planning was needed to ensure full employment, which had been adopted as an objective in both countries after the war. Many of those involved in developing mathematical models were supporters of planning, several of them, including Jacob Marshak, research director of the Cowles Commission, having been on the socialist side of the interwar debate about whether or not it was possible to have an efficient planned economy.

Support for a mixed economy was a far cry from support for Soviet-style central planning, even though the British Labour government of 1945–51 did embark on a programme of nationalizing significant parts of British industry. On the other hand, American businessmen who had dismissed the New Deal as 'socialism', had good reason to be suspicious of economists. Anti-communist hysteria in the late 1940s and early 1950s led to the charge that communism was being freely used to undermine any ideas that might be linked with planning. Many economists, including Paul Samuelson, were attacked for their views, sometimes in very strong terms. In such an environment, as Samuelson has admitted, it could be invaluable to present one's work as scientific, and the more technical, the better.

By the end of the twentieth century, this situation had changed dramatically. The views of businessmen who were innately hostile to any government action that might threaten their ability to earn profits had become much more pervasive in society. There was widespread scepticism about whether government could manage things efficiently. Along with this, there had been a broad commercialization of society, and even of values. The role of the market was extended, markets being created by government where they could not evolve spontaneously, and attempts were made to minimize the role of state-organized and state-funded economic activity. Nationalized industries were privatized; services provided by the state were outsourced to private contractors; industries were deregulated; taxes were cut, and attempts were made to reduce the level of government spending (except on defence). In Britain, a Labour Chancellor of the Exchequer felt able to urge people to celebrate high salaries rather than seeing them as a failure of the market system. Competition, markets and incentives replaced social justice as the dominant political discourse and in both the United States and Britain, inequality in the distribution of income was allowed to rise to levels that for much of the post-war era would have been considered socially divisive.

Within academic economics, two things happened. In the 1950s, economists had paid great attention to problems of market failure and how government intervention might solve them. The general approach was to work out the optimal policy, on the assumption that it could be put into practice by a government concerned with maximizing social welfare. In contrast, from the 1960s onwards, attention was increasingly paid to the possibility that government intervention might make things worse, perhaps because politicians or bureaucrats pursued their own ends, not those of society as a whole. As a result, economists increasingly developed market solutions for economic problems (such as those discussed in Chapter 2). The second change, distinct from the first, was the increasing prominence, from the 1970s on, of so-called free-market economics, or 'neoliberalism' – vigorous championing of allegedly unfettered free markets, accompanied by denunciations of government. Thus, whilst most economists still supported a considerable role for government, believing that optimal policy involved the pragmatic balancing of government and market failures, some went much further towards seeing government as the main problem. The book *Free to Choose*, by Milton and Rose Friedman (1979), together with the companion television series of the same name, served to prominently illustrate this shift in thinking: the first two topics in the PBS television series were 'The power of the market' and 'The tyranny of control'. In the 1950s, such views were regarded by most economists as extreme but, by the 1980s, though they were probably not shared by most economists, they were taken much more seriously.

In considering the factors that lay behind these changes and the role of economists in bringing them about, the distinction between economists who believe that enlarging the scope for markets is an important means for achieving social goals and economists who believe that government is inherently harmful, is important. Opposed to Friedman were many economists who held social-democratic views on the welfare state yet supported the creation of market solutions for many problems. The views of John McMillan, discussed in Chapter 1, were typical of this position. McMillan, though praising the 'reinvention of the bazaar', went on to say that markets need to be properly designed and that 'a modern economy simply cannot run on libertarian principles' (McMillan 2002, p. 226). Yet the two trends are sometimes hard to separate, as a joke that Samuelson is believed to have made about Friedman illustrates: 'Milton Friedman is like someone who knows how to spell the word 'banana' but doesn't know where to stop'. Friedman may have reached conclusions Samuelson found absurd, but his starting point was economic ideas they shared.

However, though these two changes – the greater openness of economists to market solutions and the increasing prominence of economists who were hostile to government intervention – were distinct, they interacted in ways that need to be disentangled.

LIBERTARIAN ECONOMICS

In September 1947, Friedrich von Hayek, an Austrian economist who had moved to the LSE in the 1930s, organized a meeting of people interested in developing a 'philosophy of freedom'. Its outcome was the Mont Pelerin Society (MPS), named after the location of the group's first meeting. The society's aim was not to exert an immediate influence on policy but to have a long-term influence on the climate of opinion. Hayek compared its task explicitly with that faced by the socialist and New Liberal intellectuals who had formed the Fabian Society. Although he had wanted to include more historians and philosophers, the society contained a high proportion of economists.

Milton Friedman and other members later became highly influential in the society, but Hayek was the dominant figure, mainly because of his book, *The Road to Serfdom* (1944). In this very widely read book, Hayek provided the manifesto of the new movement. In Britain, according to one commentator, Hayek's book 'succeeded in redefining the political debate ... in a way that no single book or statement of belief has done since' (Cockett 1994, p. 97). In the United States, a condensed version of *The Road to Serfdom* was published in *Reader's Digest*, which gained it a wide readership. Largely as a result of Hayek's activity, the MPS became the centre of a world-wide network that included individuals and organizations concerned with sponsoring free-market ideas, think tanks and academic economists, including many who were either members of the Chicago School or had been trained in Chicago. Amongst such organizations, the MPS was unique in the range of its contacts (including libertarians, Austrians and mainstream economists) and in the length of time over which it operated.

Whilst Hayek was preparing for the initial meeting of the MPS, he was approached by a businessman, Anthony Fisher, who had recently read *The Road to Serfdom* and wanted advice about influencing public policy for the better. Hayek's response was

I would join with others in forming a scholarly research organisation to supply intellectuals in universities, schools, journalism and broadcasting with authoritative studies of the economic theory of markets and its application to practical affairs. (quoted in Cockett 1994, p. 124)

This organization eventually materialized, in 1955, as the Institute of Economic Affairs (IEA). The IEA was, as a registered charity, Formally non-political. Its aims referred not to free markets (which might have sounded political) but to 'the study of markets and pricing systems as technical devices for registering preferences and apportioning resources' (Cockett 1994, p. 132). However, it published a series of pamphlets and books, by academic economists as well as by journalists and political figures, exploring market solutions to economic problems and advancing many ideas (such as privatization, deregulation, and methods for creating markets) that eventually became government policy. In the United Kingdom, despite its non-partisan position, it exerted a particularly strong influence on the Conservative Party under Margaret Thatcher. Beyond this, it arguably helped to change the climate of opinion by advocating policies that had previously not been taken seriously (the 'Thinking the Unthinkable' of Cockett's title) and because it providing a stream of material that, in addition to being accessible to policy makers, was attractive to students as offering applications of microeconomic theory.

In setting up the IEA, Fisher was influenced by the Foundation for Economic Education (FEE) in New York, representatives of which had been present at the initial MPS meeting), which he had visited in 1952. The FEE had been founded in 1946 by Leonard E. Read, with the support of Ludwig von Mises and the journalist Henry Hazlitt, to 'educate the world on the principles of free-market economics: individual freedom, private property, limited government and free trade'. Like the IEA, the FEE focused on retailing free-market ideas, not on academic research. The same was true of the American Enterprise Institute (AEI), founded in 1943. Education in the principles of liberty was also the aim of the Liberty Fund, established in 1960 by Pierre F. Goodrich. Goodrich was closely involved with the MPS from 1951 until his death in 1973, when he left most of his estate to the Liberty Fund, which used it to finance an extensive programme of conferences and publications.

The IEA, AEI and FEE were not the first think tanks to be formed in Britain or the United States to analyse social policy. In Britain, there was the Fabian Society (established in 1884), the National Institute for Economic and Social Research (1931) and Political and Economic Planning (1931). In the United States, there were the Russell Sage Foundation

(1907), the Brookings Institution (1916), and the NBER (National Bureau of Economic Research, established in 1920). Except for the Fabian Society, these were primarily academic research organizations. Though these groups were hardly neutral in that their work had an identifiable influence on policy, their research was based on the premise that disinterested social-scientific inquiry could, if only in the long-term, contribute to better policy making.

However, the main expansion in the number of free-market think tanks took place in the 1970s; the MPS and the IEA provided the network linking the key movers in this process. In Britain there emerged the Centre for Policy Studies (1974); the Adam Smith Institute (1977), and the Social Affairs Unit (1980), which was set up with the active support of the IEA. Fisher, the IEA's founder, was also instrumental in setting up the Canadian Fraser Institute (1975) and the International Center for Economic Policy Studies (1977), which later became the Manhattan Institute. Encouraged, Fisher in 1981 embarked on a programme to create institutes across the world with the formation of the Atlas Economic Research Foundation: 'a non-profit 501(c)(3) organization headquartered in Fairfax, Virginia, that brings freedom to the world by helping develop and strengthen a network of market-oriented think tanks that spans the globe'. Atlas's mission is 'to discover, develop and support intellectual entrepreneurs worldwide who have the potential to create independent public policy institutes and related programs, which advance our vision; and to provide ongoing support as such institutes and programs mature' (see www.atlasusa.org). At a dinner to celebrate the 30th anniversary of the IEA, Fisher referred to 'a family of 40 institutes in 20 countries' (Frost 2002, p. 161). By the end of the century, Atlas was working with or supporting 150 such bodies.

In the United States, the most important development was probably the Heritage Foundation, established in 1973. Despite the existence of the AEI, it was felt that a more aggressively conservative body was needed to influence policy and counter the efficiency with which liberal (left) ideas were translated into policy via the Brookings Institution, which was seen as part of the left's 'finely-tuned policy making machine' (Edwards 1997, pp. 2–3). The feeling became more acute after the defeat of Barry Goldwater's 1964 presidential campaign. A group centred on Strom

Thurmond and two other Republican Senators, backed by brewing magnate Joseph Coors, set up the Analysis and Research Association (ARA) in 1971, which in 1973 became the Heritage Foundation. Its President, Edwin Feulner sought to create 'a new conservative coalition that would replace the New Deal coalition which had dominated American politics for half a century' (Edwards 1997, p. 32). In 1979, Heritage designed a conservative programme that an incoming Republican administration could take up – its book of policy analysis, *Mandate for Leadership*, sold 15,000 copies in the first year. Under President Ronald Reagan, the Heritage Foundation became established in the policy-making process, its income reaching $35 million by 1997, making it larger than the much longer-established Brookings Institution.

Though Hayek's strategy was to focus on dealers in second-hand ideas, the bodies supporting this change in the think-tank landscape did not neglect academia. Until the 1960s, there had only been two significant foundations committed to explicitly free-market ideas: the Volker Fund and the Earhart Foundation. But in the 1970s, there emerged a number of other foundations that consistently supported academics who promoted free-market ideas: the Scaife Foundations, the Lynde and Harry Bradley Foundation and the John M. Olin Foundation. The resources of this group of foundations were, when compared with those of the Ford, Carnegie and Rockefeller foundations, very small but they focused, albeit not exclusively, on a small group of institutions and provided them with long-term funding that enabled them to develop, including, amongst others, the centres concerned with public choice at the Virginia Polytechnic Institute and at George Mason University and the John M.Olin Program in Law and Economics at the University of Chicago, both of which became important in the 1970s and 1980s.

THE COLD WAR

However, though some economists within the MPS (such as Friedman) became very influential within academic economics, changes in the academic arena were driven by other factors. Like most of the social sciences, economics was profoundly affected by the Second World War, which led fairly quickly into the Cold War, which in turn provided the

justification for the U.S. government to become more directly involved
in science funding: higher education, including the social sciences,
expanded massively in most countries. Government funding became
much more important, and in the United States, some of it came from
defence agencies – the U.S. Air Force, the U.S. Navy and the CIA. Philan-
thropic foundations – notably Ford, Rockefeller and Carnegie – became
major players in shaping the social sciences, at times becoming entan-
gled with the U.S. defence establishment.

One of the clearest and most important illustrations of the link between
defence funding and economics was the RAND Corporation (RAND is
short for 'research and development,' though some critics joked that it
should really be 'research and no development' on account of the amount
of purely theoretical work that it undertook), the think tank set up by the
U.S. Air Force at Santa Monica, California. Its aim was to continue the
practice, established during the war, of harnessing scientific expertise for
military purposes. RAND was important during the 1950s for its work
on game theory and the theory of rational choice, and many members
of the Cowles Commission spent time at RAND. Originally a division of
the Douglas aircraft company, undertaking research on air warfare, in
1948 RAND became independent in order to avoid conflicts of interest.
In the 1950s, it developed close links with the Ford Foundation, which
was becoming involved, along with the Carnegie and Rockefeller foundations, in consolidating U.S. influence in the world.

Under H. Rowan Gaither, its president after 1953, the Ford Foundation
pursued a policy of supporting social science 'as a tool for an expertly
managed society' (Amadae 2003, p. 38). RAND received funding alongside many universities, including Chicago. Ford's ideology of techno-
cratic management fitted RAND, a non-profit organization dominated
by scientists and engineers, perfectly. Under Gaither, who also became
Chairman of RAND's Board of Trustees, RAND became increasingly
dominated by economists centred on what came to be called 'systems
analysis'. This term denoted the techniques that could be used for efficient management within either private firms or the state. Symbolic of
the idea that efficient management systems developed in business could
also be applied to government activities was the application of systems
analysis to the conduct of the Vietnam War under Robert McNamara, a

former president of the Ford Motor Company who became secretary of defence under presidents Kennedy and Johnson.

At one level, the notion of systems analysis seems anything but ideological. However, its roots lay in rational choice theory, which arguably had an ideological use, since it provided an intellectual framework for opposing communism. The rational individual agent could be contrasted with the collective actions of the Soviet state. The key document was, it has been claimed, Arrow's *Social Choice and Individual Values* (1951) (see p. 105 above), which arose directly from his work in RAND, in 1948, when he was asked what utility function should be attributed to the Soviet Union in game theoretic analysis of nuclear strategy. Though Arrow did not view it this way, his theorem that there was no acceptable, non-dictatorial way to derive a social welfare function could be seen as answering the debate that had raged in the interwar period about socialism. Arrow showed that collectivism conflicted with liberal values. Such a strong conclusion had clear ideological implications.

An important application of rational choice theory was game theory, which was fostered by RAND because of its perceived value in developing military strategy. During the Cold War, nuclear strategy depended directly on anticipations of how the other side would respond to any moves that were made. The natural assumption was that the Russians were analysing the situation in the same way, implying that the situation could be modelled as a non-cooperative game. It is probably safe to say that, in the 1950s, the most important research on game theory was undertaken with the sponsorship of the U.S. armed forces, much of it at RAND.

But, though RAND and defence funding were important, it is important to note that they were not the only stimuli towards this vision of scientific management of the economy. For example, the Ford Foundation made the enormous investment in business schools in the 1950s. They wanted to create a new approach to business education, and to accomplish this it chose to support five 'Centres of Excellence', the main one being the GSIA at what became Carnegie-Mellon University. Here, crucial work was undertaken on finance and macroeconomics by economists who included Modigliani and Miller (see Chapter 2), and Lucas (Chapter 7). The focus was on the development and application of quantitative techniques that could be applied to management, an approach that contrasted with the case-study method practised at the more influential Harvard Business School (HBS). Although it was a business school, the GSIA's tone was set by its Dean, the economist Lee Bach, who became the author of the main rival to Samuelson's introductory economic textbook, and who worked closely with Herbert Simon, whose career spanned economics and psychology. There were dramatic differences between the theories developed at RAND and those developed by, for example, Simon at GSIA, but they had in common a commitment to being scientific through rigorous quantitative analysis.

ECONOMIC THEORY AND IDEOLOGY

Most economists would, inevitably, claim that economic ideas evolved for reasons that were not determined by ideology but by experience. The shift towards free market solutions took place because of a realization that planning and the non-market regulation of economic activity had failed. Thus Jacques Polak, perhaps the most influential economist at the IMF in the early post-war decades, observed:

The process of conversion from one [dirigiste] consensus to another [market orientated] in large areas of the world owed … [much] to the accumulating evidence of success of neoclassical policies, in particular in East Asia, contrasting with the dismal results of previous policies in so many other countries. (Polak 1997, p. 217)

Olivier Blanchard, a prominent MIT economist, has explicitly rejected, in terms that many economists would echo, the notion that economics has been driven by ideology. He wrote in the French newspaper *Libération*,

This dominance [of a certain approach to economics] means a common language and common methods. It certainly does not imply a common ideology. In fact, economics today is characterized by its pragmatism. For most of us, markets often work well but sometimes they work badly. Governments have an essential role to play. They may do this well or less well. The role of economists is to help them, case by case. There is little ideology in this. (16 October 2000; author's translation)

Thus at RAND, even though one might argue that ideology can hardly have been absent from an institution devoted to fighting the Cold War, the emphasis was on treating economic and social problems as being technical, amenable to rational analysis of evidence.

However, the charge that economists' attempts to be scientific have failed to eliminate ideological influences will not go away so easily. Joseph Stiglitz has expressed a very different view. Referring to rational-expectations models in which all agents have complete information about the world, he has written, 'That such models prevailed, especially in America's graduate schools, despite evidence to the contrary, bears testimony to a triumph of ideology over science' (*The Guardian*, 20 December 2002). This contrasts with the emphasis on the aesthetic appeal of the new theories emphasized by Buiter (discussed at the end of Chapter 7).

As will be clear from Chapters 6 and 7, since the Second World War, economics has been driven by the search for rigour, and as late as the 1990s, this was centred on modelling, most of which was based on some version of the theory of rational choice. Though economists' models had much in common, meaning that it was correct to speak of a common core of economic theory, they developed them in different ways. At Chicago there was a presumption that markets were competitive unless one had overwhelming reason to believe that they were not. It was for this reason that George Stigler (1959, p. 522), the prominent Chicago economist and MPS member claimed, 'the professional study of economics makes one politically conservative'. By 'conservative' he meant someone who wishes most economic activity to be organized by private enterprise, and believes that the forces of competition will generally hold private power in check and promote efficiency. Yet other economists did not draw this conclusion. Samuelson at MIT, Arrow at Stanford, and Tobin at Yale worked with what was essentially the same underlying theory yet reached different conclusions because they made no presumption about whether competition would hold private power in check and promote efficiency. Indeed, part of the task facing economists was to work out why the market might fail and how government might design policies to overcome these failures

Generalizations such as this are difficult to make, but it is probably correct to say that in the 1950s and for much of the 1960s, the dominant views in the economics profession were those of Samuelson, Arrow and Tobin. Friedman and Stigler were taken seriously, but Chicago was widely taken to represent an extreme view. Friedman's support of the quantity theory of money went against the dominant Keynesian consensus, and the Chicago faith in markets was considered mistaken. In the 1970s, the situation changed dramatically. The economic crisis of 1973–4, when oil prices quadrupled, involved rising unemployment and rising inflation that caused problems for conventional Keynesian models and convinced many economists that Friedman was right that there was no permanent trade-off between inflation and unemployment. That opened the way for the more rigorous macroeconomic models that Lucas and others developed during the 1970s in which demand management policy was powerless.

This change towards taking Friedman's ideas on macroeconomics more seriously paralleled the changed attitude towards other theories associated with Chicago: Gary Becker's economic analysis of the social problems from discrimination to divorce (see Chapter 6) was something of which many economists were initially sceptical, though they might admire the ingenuity of the analysis, but it gradually became something that was taken more seriously. The same was true of public choice theory, which was being developed in Virginia by Gordon Tullock and Chicago-trained economist James Buchanan. Initially thought to deal with problems that were outside economics, theories of government failure came to be more widely accepted as providing reasons that government intervention in the economy should be minimized.

Two questions arise here. The first concerns what to make of the fact that many of the economists who became influential in the 1970s had firm free-market convictions, many of them being members of the MPS, including Friedman and Becker. The second is why these ideas became so prominent when the majority of economists probably remained sceptical about them. Answering both questions requires paying attention to what economists considered rigorous theorizing and to developments discussed earlier in this chapter and Chapters 6 and 7.

There would seem little doubt that ideological commitments were a factor in the new theories (the same could of course have been said of Keynesian theories in the 1940s and 1950s), even if those involved were entirely honest in proclaiming their commitments to rigorous scientific analysis. The Chicago approach, taught to students through its workshops, involved ruthless questioning of any conclusions that did not conform with standard price theory, the basic theory of the rational consumer and competitive markets. To quote the account of one Chicago economist, Chicago's *positive* economics (its theory about how the world is, not how it ought to be)

is rooted in the hypothesis that decision makers so allocate the resources under their control that there is no alternative allocation such that any one decision maker could have his expected utility increased without a reduction occurring in the expected utility of at least one other decision maker. (Reder 1982, p. 11)

Phenomena that economists outside the tradition might have seen as demonstrating market failure or irrationality were examined until they were reconciled with this presupposition. This can be defended as a methodological position relating to what constituted rigorous economics, but it was a methodological position centred on a view of the world, namely a presupposition, or prior belief, that markets were efficient unless proved otherwise. Theory was, de facto, grounded on an ideological position.

This statement does not imply that economists elsewhere, at, for example, MIT, Stanford, Yale or Harvard, offered theories that were ideologically pure. Of course they did not. But the relationship between ideology and the search for rigour was arguably looser. Some economists might have been predisposed to favour state intervention, and they might have used techniques that reinforced that view, but there was not the same methodological imperative driving them in that direction.

These arguments extend to the new macroeconomic theories developed by Lucas. The theory of rational expectations may not have originated in Chicago, and Friedman may not have accepted it, but it was entirely consistent with Chicago methodology, in that it assumed that individuals made the best use of opportunities available to them (in this case, in processing information). The other plank of Lucas' macroeconomics, that there is equilibrium in perfectly competitive markets, was a standard Chicago assumption. What Lucas did could be presented as applying the Chicago method to macroeconomics, showing that if the world is efficient in the sense just defined, there was no role for Keynesian policies. If markets did not fail, and Keynesian theories had always been considered weak in explaining the precise reasons for this, the only reason for unemployment must be that workers or firms were making mistakes, and Lucas's model was constructed so that the only possible source of such mistakes were random, unpredictable monetary shocks. Where Keynesians might have overlooked problems of government failure, in Lucas's model, government could only interfere with the smooth operation of the economy.

If we turn to public choice theory, we find it being established not in Chicago but in Virginia, though two of the key players, Buchanan and Warren Nutter, had been trained at Chicago. The institution from which public choice emerged, the Thomas Jefferson Center for Studies in Political Economy at the University of Virginia, brought together scholars with a shared agenda: to develop a social order based on individual freedom – a clear ideological stance. Markets were their preferred form of social organization, but they realized that there was a need to study decisions that took place outside the market, which they did using the price theory they had learned at Chicago.

But though these ideas were proposed by economists predisposed to favour free markets and to be sceptical about the benefits of government intervention, why did these ideas have such an influence on the profession at large? The main reason is that they were seen as doing rigorous work in tackling important problems: for example, Tobin, a committed Keynesian, took Lucas seriously even though he disagreed profoundly with his conclusions. Even for economists who rejected his policy conclusions, Lucas opened up new ways of modelling the economy that had great appeal: in a world where inflation was changing rapidly, it was clear that expectations had, somehow, to be modelled, and any alternative to rational expectations seemed arbitrary. As for the assumption of efficient markets, there was a plethora of alternative theories. Although 'new Keynesian' theories of the labour market were taken up and widely seen as very important, especially in Europe when unemployment stayed high during the 1980s, such theories were too complicated to provide the basis for a new general theory of macroeconomics.

Politics was the other factor. The late 1970s saw the election of conservative governments on both sides of the Atlantic. At the beginning of the

1970s, President Nixon turned to Friedman, who had previously been involved with the presidential campaign of the conservative Republican Barry Goldwater. But by the time Margaret Thatcher and Ronald Reagan were elected, think tanks had become much more influential. Thatcher disliked academic economists, but had close links with the IEA and admired the work of Hayek, even though economists did not take him seriously: she was attracted by his philosophy of liberty. Her suspicion of academic economists was confirmed by a letter in which 364 of them, including some prominent figures, signed a letter to the *Times* in 1981, criticizing the economic basis for the policies she was pursuing. In the United States, Reagan, who also appreciated Hayek's work, was able to draw on policy proposals drawn up in the Heritage Foundation.

Economics changed so dramatically in the 1970s because ideological and methodological pressures were working in the same direction. There was widely perceived need to develop new theories in fields as remote as industrial organization, development economics and macroeconomics. Economists began to develop such theories using a framework that, when the complications that caused markets not to work efficiently were removed, produced conclusions that were biased towards free markets. For some economists, notably at Chicago, these conclusions were ideologically congenial. For others, the new models had the merit of being logically rigorous, simpler and theoretically more elegant than many of the older theories, and providing ample scope for generating original results. Those who were doubtful about markets found themselves on the defensive. Economists outside academia, in think tanks and in business, were offering simple solutions that had great appeal to the political classes; and within academic economics, rigorous work had become almost synonymous with explaining phenomena in terms of rational choice, the simplest models of which led, almost inexorably to free-market conclusions. Theories that justified state intervention, whether in the form of direct government provision of certain services, central planning, or macroeconomic management, were hard to justify using what had come to be considered rigorous theory, and they would be subject to relentless criticism from free-market think tanks as soon as they entered the policy arena.

9

Heterodoxy and Dissent

Even in the natural sciences, there are dissenters who reject what are generally considered well-established principles. Believers in extrasensory perception reject the laws of physics; those creationists who believe that all species were created simultaneously reject the theory of evolution; and believers in a lost civilization of Atlantis confront sceptical archaeologists and geologists. But, although scientists may feel frustrated by the publicity such views receive, the supporters of such views generally do not pose a significant problem for scientists: they can be dismissed as cranks and not taken seriously. Biologists may disagree over how evolution works, but they are in complete agreement on the principle. Archaeologists are equally unanimous that the evidence for the existence of Atlantis (at least as the city is portrayed in popular writing) is non-existent. Unorthodox ideas sometimes become respectable, but this is rare. Science is organized so as to exclude cranks. The strength of established theories is based, to a great extent, on well-established procedures and rules of evidence that rule out flawed ones. Results must be replicated in other laboratories, and they must not violate firmly established physical laws (for example, biological theories must obey the laws of chemistry). Such accepted wisdom may be closer to social conventions than objective rules than scientists would like to believe, but it has evolved because the implicit rules, however imprecise, appear to have worked over long periods of time.

The situation in economics is in some ways more like that of medicine or psychology. In medicine there are generally established views, but the understanding of many pathologies is sufficiently weak that 'alternative' theories are more likely to get a hearing than they are in the natural sciences. Many therapies are based on clinical experience of what works, and there is sometimes little understanding of the mechanisms that make them work (this knowledge often comes later). This makes it easier for purveyors of alternative therapies such as homeopathy to claim that they are successful. In addition, there is not only widespread interest in medicine but people also feel they have some expertise in it, if only as patients. Like economists, doctors are under great pressure to deliver results, and to do so quickly. It is not always possible to wait until 'science' can achieve a full understanding of a new disease before trying to do something about it. Finally, new diseases arise that require remedies (for example, AIDS or SARS). Physicists, chemists or astronomers may discover new facts that require explanation but they do not have to confront the problem that the world they are trying to explain may not be the same as it used to be. Biologists are perhaps in an intermediate position in that people feel they understand plants and animals in a way they could never understand elementary physical particles or the far reaches of the universe, and they approach biology with presuppositions about how nature works; yet there is not the same pressure for immediate results that is found in economics or medicine.

However, the parallels with medicine must not be taken too far, because in economics there is no body with the authority to rule on who is or is not qualified to practice in the profession. There is no equivalent of, say, the UK's General Medical Council or the Medical Board of California: a professional body that decides what are and are not acceptable medical practices. Professional bodies such as the AEA or the European Economic Association neither regulate membership nor determine who is qualified to speak as an economist, though the AEA has sometimes tried to do this. Thus there is no body that lays down the range of acceptable economic views. The range of acceptable views within the discipline is maintained in a decentralized way by those who control the institutions in which economists work and publish their work. For academic economists this means hiring and promotions committees and the editors of prestigious journals.

In this respect, economics is no different from other academic disciplines in that there is no need to satisfy external professional organizations. However, economics is not like natural science, where these mechanisms generally enforce a clear view of what is and is not legitimate science, nor does it fit the model of the social sciences, such as psychology, sociology and political science, where much greater pluralism is accepted. In contrast, economics has a strong disciplinary identity, but it lacks the degree of consensus that characterizes the natural sciences. While there is considerable agreement that economics should be rigorous, and even though fashions change, there is considerable agreement on what rigour should consist of. Despite this, fundamental disagreements remain. Some of these, such as disputes between Keynesians and RBC theorists or between those who pursue pure theory and those who favour inductive statistical work, are accepted in that the leading journals will publish both sides of the arguments. However, differences sometimes become so great that an economist comes to be seen as an outsider – a dissenter or heretic in relation to the views generally held in the profession. This may be out of a choice or because their work is not taken seriously, usually because it is not seen as sufficiently rigorous. Some economists have perceived themselves to be sufficiently marginalized that they have set up their own organizations to discuss and promote their work. The result is that there is a set of approaches, albeit one with very fuzzy boundaries that change all the time, that can be found in the top journals and leading university departments, variously referred to as the 'orthodoxy' or, less critically, 'the mainstream', as well as groups of economists, publishing in other outlets, who do not fit in.

In many cases, this marginalization has had ideological dimensions. Marxian economics, radical economics and Post-Keynesian economics have leaned squarely to the left, seeing capitalism as having failed in one way or another. Austrians, on the other hand, with their hostility to government intervention, lean the other way. More important, however, has probably been the rejection of what are seen as orthodox ways of doing economics, notably rejection of the formal modelling by which most economists have sought to establish the scientific status of their discipline.

THE RHETORIC OF KEYNESIAN REVOLUTION

Keynes was the economist who made dissent, or heterodoxy, respectable. In *The General Theory of Employment, Interest and Money* (1936), Keynes wrote of a long struggle to escape from 'habitual modes of thought and expression' (Keynes 1936, p. xiii). He praised

the brave army of heretics ... who, following their intuitions, have preferred to see the truth obscurely and imperfectly rather than to maintain error, reached indeed with clearness and consistency and by easy logic but on hypotheses inappropriate to the facts. (ibid., p. 371)

Academic economists had generally treated these economists as cranks, not worth taking seriously. Keynes conceded that much of their work was flawed and that their reasoning was illogical. However, as the quotation shows, he also thought that their intuition was correct and that this was more important than the flaws in their reasoning. He could get away with such a remark because his credentials as one of the leading monetary economists of his day were never in doubt.

After the Keynesian revolution, most economists took on board Keynes's arguments about aggregate demand, but they did not draw the conclusion that being correct was more important than being logically rigorous. On the contrary, logical rigor was increasingly seen as the only way to avoid error. Ironically, though Keynes had praised heresy (at least this one heresy), his ideas helped establish a more dominant macro-economic orthodoxy than existed before 1936: within a few years of his book's publication, the victory of Keynesianism was virtually complete. When Milton Friedman and fellow monetarists tried to reinstate the quantity theory of money, they were challenging the consensus.

Though Keynes would never have wished to see a new orthodoxy established, his rhetorical style contributed to this outcome. He adopted what has been described as an oppositional style, positioning his ideas against something he called 'classical economics', which summed up the habitual modes of thought from which he was trying to escape. Rather than engage seriously with the variety of interwar ideas on unemployment and the business cycle, he grouped them together and dismissed them. Another factor that contributed to this apparently dramatic break was that Keynesian ideas were taken up by the new generation of economists, who used them as the basis for the mathematical models that rapidly became more rigorous than anything that was found in the pre-war literature (see Chapter 7). This was further reinforced by the use of national income statistics that hardly existed before 1936. The result was that, even though Keynes own work was firmly rooted in the literature of the 1930s, to economists trained on the Keynesian models of the late 1940s and the 1950s, the literature of the 1930s, which was largely based on verbal reasoning, seemed inconsequential and lacking in rigour.

Keynes's rhetoric also encouraged economists to argue in terms of competing schools of thought. In the 1940s and 1950s, economists debated 'Keynes versus the classics'. In the 1970s, it was 'monetarism versus Keynesianism'. In the 1980s, it was 'new classical macroeconomics' or 'real business cycle theory' versus 'new Keynesian' macroeconomics. Keynes was not responsible for these differences of opinion, but he established a highly influential precedent for arguing in such terms. It made it easier for economists to see their subject in terms of what philosopher of science Thomas Kuhn, in the 1960s, called competing paradigms, each embodying a different view of the world.

DISSENT BEFORE THE 1970S

In the immediate post-war era, it was the libertarians who were on the defensive due to the ascent of Keynesian ideas and, more generally, the expansion in the role of government that came with the New Deal and the Second World War. In the early 1940s, Hayek wrote:

If it is no longer fashionable to emphasize that 'we are all socialists now', this is so merely because the fact is too obvious. Scarcely anybody doubts that we must continue to move towards socialism. (Hayek 1944, p. 3)

That was the background to the MPS (discussed in Chapter 8): Hayek believed that liberalism needed to be defended against collectivism. However, most economist members of the MPS were very much a part of the profession they were trying to change (leaving aside Hayek who, though an economist, had moved into other fields after his ideas were eclipsed by Keynes's *General Theory*). When Stigler and Friedman in the 1950s and 1960s tried to make the case for free-market economics and the quantity theory of money (which became the basis for monetarism), they were trying to change economics. They made use of traditional economic theory, arguing that those who supported state intervention in the economy were not applying it sufficiently rigorously.

Their theories were highly orthodox even though they applied them in novel ways.

The most influential economist to portray himself as a dissenter during this period exemplified the socialist tendencies decried by Hayek: John Kenneth Galbraith. During the war he had, while working in the Office of Price Administration, been instrumental in running the United States as a planned economy through controlling prices. In a series of books, *American Capitalism* (1952), *The Affluent Society* (1957), and *The New Industrial State* (1967), he offered visions of an American capitalist society that were sharply opposed to those of many economists. The building blocks of his theory were in many ways very orthodox. For example, his argument that firms did not maximize profits but pursued goals, such as sales maximization, that reflected the needs of what he called the 'technostructure' was of a piece with the managerial theories of the firm that more conventional economists were developing. However, he spurned technical details, let alone mathematical modelling, choosing instead to address his work to the general public. His high public profile, both as a journalist and within the Democratic Party, and the success of his books with the general public drew him away from an economics profession in which the use of mathematical techniques was becoming increasingly important. The result was that by the 1960s he increasingly identified himself, and was seen by others, as more and more of a dissenter.

Some dissenters, including Marxists, found life difficult not so much because their economics was unorthodox as because their suspected association with the Communist Party could be used to force them out of their posts. Others who are now considered dissenters prospered within the system. However, though the Cambridge Keynesians Joan Robinson and Nicholas Kaldor, later considered heterodox economists, might have disagreed with ideas that the profession at large took for granted, they still published in the same journals and debated with their more orthodox counterparts such as Samuelson, Solow and Friedman.

What changed the situation, bringing together radical critics of the status quo, was the escalation of the Vietnam War in the mid-1960s. This came on top of a growing awareness that two decades of growth had failed to eliminate poverty and an increasing consciousness of widespread discrimination against ethnic minorities and women. McCarthyism was gone, higher education had expanded even further, and students were freer to express dissent than they had been a decade earlier.

In economics, the decisive event was the response of the AEA to the Chicago police department's treatment of demonstrators at the 1968 Democratic convention. Protestors had tried to move the following year's AEA meeting away from Chicago but, unlike some other social science organizations caught in the same position, the AEA decided to stay. The association simply issued a statement that staying in Chicago did not imply support for what had happened. The result was that in 1969, while the AEA was meeting in Chicago, a few hundred protestors attended a breakaway meeting in Philadelphia, joining the recently formed Union for Radical Political Economy (URPE). URPE took many ideas from Marxism, but its approach was broader, its defining feature being a focus on issues related to inequality, poverty, race, discrimination and structures of power within the economy. It was a radical, dissenting group.

PARADIGMS AND THE EMERGENCE OF 'HETERODOX' ECONOMICS

On the whole, economists pay little attention to philosophy. However, the way economics evolved in the 1970s cannot be understood without referring to the work of one philosopher-cum-historian of science, Thomas Kuhn. Kuhn's *The Structure of Scientific Revolutions* (1962/1970) challenged the widely held view that science developed in a cumulative progress. He claimed instead that science involved periods of 'normal science', during which scientists' view of the world was formed by the ruling 'paradigm', and other periods in which anomalies provoked qualitative change. In a period of normal science, the basic laws of science are not questioned – they are considered to have been securely established – and scientific activity consists of applying the paradigm to new problems, extending it, and fixing any problems that arise. The classic example was Newtonian physics. It is only cranks (or science-fiction writers) who suggest that objects may move faster than the speed of light or that perpetual motion machines are possible.

In any period of normal science, there are inconsistencies and phenomena that the theory cannot explain. If they relate to things that do not matter, they can be ignored. Sometimes anomalies are more central (such as the apparent incompatibility of wave and corpuscular theories of light), but scientists work with the theories anyway on the grounds that they will eventually be resolved. Sometimes, however, anomalies become serious, forcing scientists to reconsider the paradigm. If this happens, a crisis may develop, in which scientists look around, sometimes randomly, or turn to philosophy until they find a resolution. This is how a new paradigm emerges – through a scientific revolution.

What made Kuhn's theory of interest to economists who were dissatisfied with the status quo was his argument that, when a scientific revolution took place, the old and new paradigms might be incommensurable. Because they did not answer the same questions, it might be impossible to say, categorically, that one was better than another. They were just different. Talk of a 'crisis in economics' was widespread in the mid-1970s as the subject appeared to be floundering in the wake of the oil-price shocks, the productivity slowdown and stagflation; from there it was but a short step to the argument that economics needed a new paradigm.

One group that sought consciously to create a new paradigm in economics came to be labelled Post-Keynesian economics. Two young American economists argued this in an article in the very prominent *Journal of Economic Literature* (the AEA's abstracting journal, received by all its members), 'An Essay on Post-Keynesian Theory: A New Paradigm in Economics' (Eichner and Kregel 1975). One of the authors, Jan Kregel, had been explicit in using the idea of incommensurability to defend the new paradigm:

Looking at an abstract figure, I may be able to see the outlines of a rabbit. Someone else, looking at the very same abstract figure, may believe it to be an elephant. But for me to see the elephant implies losing the rabbit; both cannot be seen at once. So it seems also with economic theory. ... So I ask you to do your best to try and see my rabbit ... Afterwards, if you still prefer the elephant (or in turn find a duck) you are welcome to it. (Kregel 1973, p. 4)

The new paradigm involved the same pieces as the old one, but they formed a new picture that could not be seen without abandoning the old one.

The significance of this movement for the argument being made here lies not in the ideas it represented so much as in the fact that the

Post-Keynesians were creating a self-consciously heterodox group within the economics profession. They were disillusioned with the way they were treated, feeling that they could not get papers accepted at the AEA meetings or published in leading journals. They concluded that they had to set up their own organization and journal. They had strong affinities with the economists who had formed URPE in 1968 but were a loosely defined group. As Post–Keynesianism evolved and different groups contended for influence, there was a series of attempts to define what Post-Keynesian economics was. Some of their more orthodox critics, such as Nobel Laureate Robert Solow, a leading economist at MIT, picked up on this.

I don't see an intellectual connection between a Hyman Minsky ... and someone like Alfred Eichner ... except that they are all against the same thing, namely the mainstream, whatever that is ... It [Post-Keynesian economics] seems to be mostly a community which knows what it is against, but doesn't offer anything very systematic that could be described as a positive theory. (Klamer 1984, pp. 137–8)

Against this, some Post-Keynesians, such as Geoffrey Harcourt, argued that this was a virtue, indicating an open-minded, pluralistic approach.

Another group that emerged in the 1970s advocated what came to be called 'Austrian' economics. A conference in 1974 brought together a group of economists who found inspiration in the work of the Austrian School that traced its origins to Carl Menger, an economist based in Vienna in the late nineteenth-century. Though this tradition was originally located in Austria, in the 1930s, many of its members had been forced to leave Austria and ended up in the United States. Most of these emigrés were integrated into the mainstream of American economics even if they retained distinctive views (outstanding examples being Joseph Schumpeter, Fritz Machlup and Gottfried Haberler), but some reacted against the orthodoxy that had emerged from the 1950s onwards. Hayek, Ludwig Lachmann and Murray Rothbard were the most significant figures in this movement. They and their American followers formed the core of what became, from the 1970s, an organized dissenting group.

The Austrians were at the other end of the political spectrum from the Post-Keynesians and the radicals of URPE, but they shared the belief that their ideas were unwelcome in the profession as a whole and that they needed to organize if their ideas were to survive. This view was also held by the group that formed the Public Choice Society and other groups that had begun to form at this time. Whereas public choice economists, who employed many orthodox techniques (notably, the technique of modelling agents as utility maximizers), managed to bring the analysis of non-market decision making into the mainstream within about a decade, other dissenting groups remained marginalized, though the award of the Nobel memorial prize to Hayek made Austrians more prominent. Although heterodox groups remained very small relative to total size of the economics profession, they survived. Their heterodox identity and their claim that advocating pluralism was what differentiated them from the allegedly monolithic orthodoxy was important to many heterodox economists. This is shown by the establishment in 1993 of the International Confederation of Associations for Pluralism in Economics and, in 1998, of the Association of Heterodox Economics. The latter brought together dissenters who would previously have been opposed to each other. This move towards pluralism was echoed in the appeals for pluralism associated with the Post–Autistic Economics movement, discussed in Chapter 1).

ORTHODOXY AND HETERODOXY IN ECONOMICS

Heterodox groups in modern economics, whose members consciously present themselves as offering an alternative to the dominant way of doing economics, have core beliefs that they believe to be fundamentally different from the conventional ones. These core beliefs are buttressed by their accounts of their historical roots. Post-Keynesians tell the story of how the radical elements in the *General Theory* were ignored or neutralized by Hicks, Samuelson and the architects of the neoclassical synthesis (see Chapter 7). The original, more radical Keynesianism was kept alive by a small minority whose ideas formed the basis for post-Keynesian economics. Austrians claim that Austrian economics was always distinct from the mainstream, its various branches going back to a common source in Menger. Others trace their ancestry back to Marx, Thorstein Veblen or find it in sociology. These accounts have some justification. However, they ignore the extent to which the progenitors of these heterodoxies were, at one time, within the mainstream of economic thought as it then was. Heterodoxy, as it now exists, comprising comparatively small groups that are substantially isolated from the bulk of the profession, is a phenomenon that is of relatively recent origin, going back only to the late 1960s.

Another aspect of the problem is that, especially in an age where fields are proliferating within economics, there is considerable dissent within the mainstream. An analogy can perhaps be made with Protestant Christianity in Britain. In addition to dissenters (Baptists, Congregationalists, Methodists, Quakers and so on) who are outside the Church of England, there are opposing groups within the established church. The Church of England includes evangelicals, liberals and Anglo-Catholics who, despite periodic outbreaks of hostility, manage to remain within the same organization. Thus, experimental economics, represented by the Economic Science Association established in 1986 is unorthodox yet increasingly within the mainstream. In the growing literature on transaction cost economics (the so-called New Institutional Economics) one finds assumptions that are very different from those in the standard textbooks. MIT trained Nobel Laureate, Joseph Stiglitz, whose career has taken him through many of the world's top university economics departments, must be considered as a mainstream economist, and yet he has legitimately presented himself as dissenting from the prevailing view of how markets operate. The picture of mainstream economics could easily be painted as one of fragmentation, for new approaches to the subject are proliferating.

The difference between these two types of dissent is twofold. First, heterodox economists have made a choice to stand outside the mainstream of the profession, rejecting the orthodoxy they criticize to an extent that those who remain insiders have not. Second, heterodox economics generally lies outside the bounds of what is considered legitimate analysis. This is not always so because economists may choose to identify themselves as heterodox, even though the nature of their work does not require them to do this. The boundaries of what is generally considered legitimate economics may be changing, allowing a considerable diversity of approaches, and very blurred indeed (which, in part, reflects the change that is taking place), but there are limits to what is considered acceptable. These limits are set by the editors and referees of the core journals and thus are nowhere codified; theses limits probably can not be codified because those setting them often disagree sharply among themselves. It seems very likely that those limits were tightened in the 1970s as formal modelling was applied to an increasing range of phenomena, thereby provoking the formation of the groups discussed in this chapter.

Heterodox economists frequently make two charges against their orthodox colleagues. The first is that ignoring their work means ignoring insights that are fundamental to understanding economic phenomena. The second is that the economics profession adopts an excessively narrow view of the methods that should be used in economics and that it needs to be more pluralist, the claim made by the Post-Autistic Economics movement discussed in Chapter 1. The response to both these claims is that 'insights' about the economy are rarely useful unless economists also have tools with which to apply those insights. Moreover, where hetero-dox economists see only uniformity, it is possible to point to the way in which mainstream economics has, especially in the last decade, become open to new ideas about where to find data and on how to do applied work. Within the mainstream there is great suspicion of methodological claims that are not backed up by results. This does not mean that eco-nomics should not be more pluralist (on the contrary, it was argued at the end of Chapter 7 that the dominance of the DSGE model may have caused problems in macroeconomics). Rather, it means that arguments about pluralism are more persuasive if they arise from examples of how new insights and methods can solve important problems. In Chapter 10, it is argued that such work has come as much from economists with impeccable orthodox credentials as from those who describe themselves as heterodox.

PART III

EVALUATION

Running through all the four chapters in Part II are questions of methodology. What does it mean to be scientific in economics or, to put the question differently, how can economic inquiry best be carried out? The abstract theories and elaborate statistical methods that have been the butt of so much criticism were the result of economists' having attempted to construct a rigorous scientific economics. Given the mixed record of success and failure revealed in Part I, what lessons can be drawn? Rather than answer this question by proposing a new methodology that will solve these problems, Chapter 10 suggests that the value of formal theory may not lie in presenting a view of how the world must work but in continually questioning our presuppositions about how the economic world operates. This offers a path between complete scepticism about economic theory and formal econometric methods and uncritical acceptance of the reigning orthodoxies. To support this case, the chapter starts with an exploration of the different ways in which economic knowledge can be created.

10

Economic Science and Economic Myth

One of the main reasons economics receives so much criticism is that much economic reasoning is based on what can best be called common sense. Not only do economic theories deal with everyday phenomena, such as households, firms and markets, but many of the mechanisms that economists analyse are familiar from everyday experience. It should not take training in economics to figure out that if there is a shortage of something, its price is likely to rise, or that it is riskier to hold stock in a single company than to hold a diversified portfolio. Technical economics appears often to be formalizing common sense ideas and either proving what does not need to be proved (because it is obvious) or losing track of reality as economists make the abstractions necessary to apply their formal techniques. So the question 'What do economists know?' is about method: 'How do the techniques available to economists produce knowledge that goes beyond that which is clear using common sense?'

The obvious way to create economic knowledge is to create statistics. Everyone knows about the prices of toothpaste, bread, strawberries, mobile phone contracts, and the myriad of products that we consume, but without systematic analysis it is impossible to see what is happening to prices as a whole. Thanks to government statisticians, we can attach a number to the rate of inflation or the price level. There exist measures, such as the Retail Price Index, the Consumer Price Index and the GDP deflator (the price index derived from comparing gross domestic product with what it would be if everything were valued in a given base period's prices) that can tell us what inflation is. Some economic statistics can be described as 'natural' measurements: the number of tons of steel produced in the EU in 2007 is straightforward, as is the total value of woollen textile exports from the United Kingdom. Such statistics may be the by-product of normal government activities, perhaps as a result of collecting taxes.

Other statistics involve a more substantial conceptual input in which economists play a significant role. A concept such as national income may sound simple, but it results from a series of decisions about what incomes are to be included and how they are to be calculated. A measure such as GDP is part of a system that derives its rationale from theories about how the economy works. A good example is the contrast between Western measures such as GDP and the measures used in the former Soviet bloc, which centred on 'material product': the value of services, such as banking or entertainment, was not recognized. Soviet measures were based on Marxist economic theory, Western ones on Keynesian theory, and the result was different ways of measuring income.

However, statistics by themselves are very limited. It is all very well to measure economic quantities, but to understand what is going on in the economy, we need to know something about the relationships between economic quantities – about the causal mechanisms that are at work. It is here that we get to the heart of the disagreements between economists. Induction is one approach. At its simplest, induction involves searching for patterns in the data and then trying to explain these patterns – a 'bottom-up' approach. The opposite approach is deduction: we start with assumptions about the causal mechanisms operating in the economy and use logical inference to work out the consequences of these assumptions. In short, we construct an economic theory. As philosophers have shown, these are no more than idealized cases at opposite ends of a spectrum; in practice there are fundamental problems with both. Induction requires a theory, if only a primitive one, because we need to make decisions about what to observe and what to ignore. Conversely, deduction requires some material to which logical analysis can be applied. However, induction and deduction are useful categories for thinking about the way economists argue, marking out a spectrum along which economists occupy different places.

The conventional view among economists is that theories should be based on assumptions about how individuals behave. Households, firms, governments and other organizations are made up of individuals, and therefore if one can explain the behaviour of individuals one must be able to explain how the organizations behave. This argument applies *a fortiori* if countries are considered as a whole. As explained in Chapters 6 and 7, the most common assumption about individual behaviour is that people are rational in a very precisely defined sense (which is not synonymous with the meaning of rationality in everyday speech). It is that, when faced with a choice, people know what they prefer and choose accordingly. This means that, unless people's preferences change, observed behaviour will be consistent and that generalizations can be made about what people will do in particular circumstances. By formulating this theory using mathematics, describing behaviour either by sets of equations or diagrams, it is possible to predict how choices will change when people are faced with changes in the prices of goods they buy or in their income. Sometimes the mathematics will produce seemingly obvious results (which might be taken as confirming that the theory is correct). But sometimes it produces results that would have been very difficult to derive without the mathematics, and that might even be counter-intuitive.

What are the problems with this approach? The obvious ones are that people may not be rational, or even if they are rational, it is not clear what rationality means. Take the labour market as an example. Some economists take the view that the only legitimate way to model labour supply is as the result of rational choice in a competitive market, which means that unemployment must be voluntary. Others economists take involuntary unemployment as a reality and consider it better to make a seemingly ad hoc assumption, such as that wages do not fall in response to unemployment, as a better way to describe how the labour market works. Such an assumption fails to explain the problem of the labour market, but if the assumption is good enough, it makes it possible to analyse other problems.

Because this is an important point, consider two more examples. Suppose an economist is trying to construct a theory about innovation – about the resources firms will allocate to investment in research and development (R&D). This model may require knowledge of how the firm sets its prices day-by-day. However, the economist may not know enough about the market to be able to say what the rational, profit-maximizing price will be, and may simply assume that price to be a fraction of the average production cost. Such an assumption about price setting is ad hoc in the sense that it does not follow from rational behaviour, but it may be adequate for analysing the problem of R&D expenditure. Perhaps the most famous example of this type of theorizing is Keynes. In 1936, he based his theory of unemployment on the assumption that as people got richer, they would save a higher proportion of their income. This did not contradict the assumption of rationality but was an empirical generaliza-tion, based on his intuitions.

This means that economic theory can be approached in different ways. The case for pure theory was made by Robbins in 1932 (see Chapter 6). He argued that the whole of economic theory could be derived from the assumption that resources were scarce and that choices needed to be made about how to use them. Indeed, he considered this assumption so basic that it defined what economics was. In contrast, other economic theorists have argued that economic theories must start from a range of assumptions, chosen to reflect what are believed to be important features of the economic world, and that empirical work is needed to decide on the assumptions that should be used for tackling different problems. The purist approach advocated by Robbins does not work in practice because the economic world is complicated, and there is too much that we do not understand.

Econometrics, as the term is now understood, is about the analysis of economic data using formal statistical methods. This type of empiri-cal work is, by definition, mathematical and is constrained by both the mathematical models that econometricians know how to handle and by the statistics that are available to them. Typically, both are far less than perfect. As in economic theory, there are different approaches to econometric work, often related to the uses of different types of data. One view is that econometrics should be inductive – that the first task of the econometrician is to provide an empirical model, or statistical sum-mary, of the data. The opposing view is that the econometrician should start with an economic theory, and then use data to test whether or not the theory is a satisfactory fit. There are also, as in economic theory, differences of opinion over the importance of rigour. The purist position is that it is important to use best-practice statistical techniques, even if this means that using an economic model is simpler than one would wish. Otherwise, any results will be problematic. Against this is the view that econometricians must do the best they can with such data as are available, and that where data are limited, it may be sufficient to use simple techniques, as long as one remains aware that the results have to be used with caution. Using rigorous statistical methods can never make up for having an inadequate model or unreliable data.

Some economists even go so far as to reject econometrics altogether, preferring the informal use of statistics, perhaps loosely guided by economic theories, that are found in many historical explanations. These are reasoned arguments, but they are not conducted with the logical rigour found in a mathematical argument. Historical explanations of historical phenomena, such as the Great Depression of the 1930s or Britain's forced expulsion from the European Exchange Rate Mechanism in 1992, are explained using statistics, evidence about how policy makers thought about events at the time, knowledge based on comparable earlier episodes, beliefs about how people form expectations, about how panic sets in and so on. The resulting picture of events is far more complicated than the econometrician's representation of what was happening but is developed less rigorously. Others have turned to new types of evidence, including experiments, brain scans and studies of behaviour in non-economic settings.

In an ideal world, these methods would fit together perfectly. The economic theory used to tackle a particular problem would be a component of a larger model of economic activity as a whole, and would rest on a fully consistent theory of how all individuals in the economy behave. It would be tested using state-of-the-art statistical methods, and the empirical models would be consistent with all the available data. However, the real world is not like that – it is too complicated to be encompassed by a single theory, and the data are far too limited. The result is that economists have to tackle problems in different ways, using different methods to cut through the messiness of the real world. Sometimes it may be necessary to work with highly abstract models, based on assumptions that are blatantly unrealistic, in order to discover anything about mechanisms that may be operating in the real world. For other problems, it may be more fruitful to argue less rigorously in order to keep in closer touch with real-world facts. This creates a variety of types of knowledge: theoretical propositions, some derived rigorously from assumptions about individual behaviour, others from generalizations that are believed to describe the world, and empirical propositions ranging from predictions derived from statistically-rigorous modelling to simple generalizations based on looking at tables and graphs. Alongside all these, of course, are what might be called common-sense observations about the world, such as knowledge of economic institutions and how they operate or simple observations of things that are obvious – such as that households have widely different incomes and behaviour patterns.

TESTING ECONOMIC THEORIES

In natural science, scientific laws are generally established through controlled experiment. Steel balls are timed falling from towers, gases are put under pressure and the changes in temperature are measured and so on. However, even with the immensely powerful experimental and observational methods available to natural scientists, it is difficult to test any scientific theory conclusively because if the evidence does not fit, it is impossible to be sure whether the theory is wrong or whether there is a problem with the test. A related problem is that even though testing may indicate that a theory should be rejected, that theory may remain the best starting point for the construction of new theories. A theory may fail but form an essential part of a research programme that offers more prospect of success than any alternative. Though philosophers have tried to formalize this, it is in practice a matter of making informed judgements that cannot be reduced to any simple decision rule.

In economics there is the further problem that doubts about data are often a major reason economists are often more sceptical about empirical results than are natural scientists. Much economic data derives from statistics collected for other purposes and does not always measure exactly what is wanted. Take an important economic concept: profits. Accountants calculate the profits earned by almost every firm. It is necessary to know what a firm's profits are in order to calculate its tax liabilities; profits also provide investors with information about the firms' performance. Depending on the situation, the accountants may have an incentive to maximize or minimize the figure. In either case, the way accountants measure profits is not necessarily the one that the economist is interested in. This is one reason economists have tried to develop new data sources and methods. Nevertheless, the economist may have no choice but to work with statistics that accountants have collected, even though they may not be defined in precisely the correct way. This is just one of many possible examples. Accounting data will rarely reflect illegal activities, whereas the economist would often wish to include them. The economist may also need to capture activities that, though legal, are simply not properly recorded in sets of accounts.

Thus when economists test theories, the results are often inconclusive. Sometimes this is because they have not used the right data. It can also be a problem when there are too few observations to estimate models precisely, perhaps because the government has only recently started compiling statistics in a given area or because definitions have changed. For example, the UK definition of unemployment – how it is measured – changed eight times between 1979 and 1990, Mrs. Thatcher's term of office, reducing the number of people classified as unemployed by over 500,000. Most of these changes were the result of practical administrative arrangements, not a deliberate attempt to massage the figures, but this illustrates the kinds of problems that lie beneath even apparently simple statistics. And this may be an extreme example, but the general problem is pervasive. Furthermore, even if the data is reliable and measures what needs to be measured, theory is rarely sufficiently precise to permit any single test to be decisive. For example, even if theory tells us that a rise in income will be followed by an increase in consumption, it will not tell us how soon that increase in consumption will take place. In other words, economic theory does not usually specify the 'lags' involved. This makes testing difficult.

However, even if statistical methods could establish incontrovertibly that certain relationships could be found in the data, one cannot always know whether those relationships will prove reliable enough to form the basis for theorizing. For example, it was for a long time believed that the proportion of national income being paid as wages was stable, so much so that some economists considered it a constant. The same was true of the ratio of capital stock (the value of buildings, machinery, vehicles and so on) to output. Some economists used these 'constants' as starting points in theories of growth. Other economists maintained that, even if they had been stable in the past, there could be no guarantee that they would remain so if economic conditions changed. Any theory that will continue to work even in changed economic conditions must be based on relationships that are not going to change, which for some economists means individuals' preferences and technology. This was the basis for the Lucas critique of stabilization policy discussed in Chapter 7.

Economists do not just want to find reliable patterns in economic data – they also want to know what causes what. Where can they get evidence relating to causes? One place is the laboratory, where the factors in experiments can be controlled. However, given the problems with social science experiments, it is often more persuasive to look instead at actions in the real world – at what has happened when governments have intervened in the economy, or after some shock has taken place. This means going beyond statistical information to evidence that often follows directly from common sense. Notwithstanding the problem of man-made climate change, it is generally clear that the weather is an exogenous shock, so if a cold summer causes a bad harvest we know that causation runs from weather to wheat yields and not vice versa. At another level, it is possible to conclude that certain policy changes may be considered external shocks to the system that have a causal effect on economic variables. An examination of the minutes of the Federal Open Markets Committee or the Bank of England's MPC (Monetary Policy Committee) may show why decisions were taken and provide evidence on causation.

The discussion so far has presumed that good theories require accurate assumptions, whether these are based on empirical regularities or knowledge, perhaps based on introspection, of how people behave. Against this, it has been claimed that assumptions need not be accurate and that as a result it is pointless to try to judge theories by the realism of their assumptions (see Chapter 6). Theories are useful because they generate predictions, which is how they should be tested. A powerful theory is based on very small number of assumptions but nonetheless successfully predicts a large variety of phenomena. Many economists would argue that the theory of supply and demand is very simple, and that it successfully predicts a great deal. It predicts that if a tax is imposed on a product, the price will rise by an amount that depends on demand and supply conditions. It predicts that rent controls will typically lead to shortages of rented housing. It predicts that the prices of certain agricultural products will fluctuate much more than those of most manufactured products. Thus, even if the theory of supply and demand cannot be tested directly, there is a weight of evidence in its favour, at least under certain circumstances.

This belief that economics should be judged by its predictions is one reason why some economists challenge the long-held belief that experimental methods cannot be applied in the social sciences, and who derive what they see as hard evidence from experimentation on human subjects. Like natural scientists and psychologists, economists can have their laboratories, where they conduct experiments on human subjects (or even non-human subjects, such as mice or pigeons though this is far more controversial). One of the attractions of such methods is that they may reveal behaviour patterns that could not be predicted using economic theory, and that it is possible to create 'behavioural' economics using such information. The result is that if behaviour does deviate from what is suggested by rational choice, the economist can still analyse it.

Such methods have become much more widely accepted than was the case even twenty years ago, but doubts remain about what some experiments reveal about behaviour outside the laboratory. Because they know that they are playing games (even if they involve 'real' money), subjects in the economist's laboratory may well behave differently from the way economic agents behave in the real world. Perhaps more significantly, though behavioural economists have produced many examples of behaviour that cannot be explained using rational choice, and though these anomalies may be important, it is not always clear how they should be incorporated into economic models.

A successful scientific theory will stand up to rigorous scrutiny. It generally must be consistent with other accepted theories; able to explain existing evidence, whether from observing the world directly or from experiments, and enable scientists to design new experiments that produce results that the theory predicts. The precise meaning of success

varies according to the context. In physics, the mathematical formula-
tion of the theory and its relation to other theories is important. It is not
an absolute requirement that theories are consistent with each other, but
when this is not the case (for example, with wave and particle theories of
light) it is considered to be a problem, or at least a puzzle that may lead to
further work and yield fresh insights. Being able to produce experimental results that support the theory and are inconsistent with, and hence
refute, competing theories is also important.

Though it has been questioned whether his results did in fact bear
the interpretation placed on them, the experiments by which Edding-
ton tested Einstein's theory of relativity are an example of this. Einstein's
theory predicted that gravity would bend the path of light, something
that would not happen under Newton's theory. Measuring the positions
of stars when they were almost behind the sun at the time of an eclipse
(without which it would have been impossible to see them) was taken
to show that the theory of relativity was correct. In contrast, success in
medicine means curing patients' illnesses or, at least, alleviating their
suffering, thereby improving the length and quality of their lives. Knowing why medicines work is important; it leads to further progress and
makes it easier to avoid undesirable side effects, but it is not essential and
not always possible.

These problems are even more pervasive in economics. As was
explained in Chapters 6 and 7, the scope and rigour of economic theory
have increased dramatically since the 1960s, and empirical methods have
reached a degree of sophistication that was unimaginable a half century
ago. Yet, the complexity of the real world means that such methods have
limitations and, as a result, formal methods have to be combined with
less formal ones. Most economics involves not the mechanical application of 'pure' methods but brings together results obtained by different
methods to reach a persuasive conclusion, not because the logic is compelling but because of the overall weight of evidence. This 'informal' use
of a range of evidence to support economic ideas rather than a decisive,
methodologically simple test is inevitable given the complexity of what
economists claim to know.

Economic theory and the various empirical methods used by economists clearly have limitations in that they cannot on their own establish

decisively that the conclusions reached in formal models are correct. This problem has led many economists to be sceptical about the link between models and understanding reality, and this scepticism extends to both economic theory and econometric work. On economic theory, many would echo the following critique:

> More often than not, the method of economics consists either of the application of an existing theory with little attention to whether it is closely related to the system being considered or, worse still, of recommending that the system be changed to bring it into conformity with the assumptions of theory. (Phillips 1962, p. 361)

On econometrics, Lawrence Summers has argued that simple, robust empirical generalizations have been far more influential than formal econometric work (though he himself has engaged in such work). In a similar vein, two econometricians challenged readers of the *Journal of Econometrics* 'to name a paper that contains significance tests which significantly changed the way economists think about some economic proposition' (Keuzenkamp and Magnus 1995, p. 21). They failed to elicit the flood of examples that one would expect if economics were as successful as is often claimed.

At one level these critics are correct. The precise coefficients produced by econometric work, irrespective of the data sources used, rarely have a long-lasting effect on economic theory. The world changes, and they become out of date, which means that economists are not interested in precise numbers so much as whether effects are positive or negative, or significantly different from zero. Precise numerical quantitative relationships are important at a particular time and place, whereas it is qualitative relationships or approximate quantitative ones that matter over longer periods. But in a more important sense they are wrong. Whilst precise coefficients may not matter, econometric results contribute to the weight of evidence that causes economists to change their minds. The developments in macroeconomics during the 1970s (discussed in Chapter 7) illustrate this very clearly. There were many attempts to estimate the relationship between inflation and unemployment (so-called Phillips curves) and though every one of these studies was ephemeral, this work contributed to the evidence that led economists to accept that, as Friedman and Phelps had argued, expectations of inflation had to be taken into account. Similarly, few economists nowadays will recall the individual studies that tested Lucas's monetary shocks theory of the cycle, but such work was influential in turning economists towards RBC theories in the early 1980s. Again, the convergence between RBC and new Keynesian models in the 1990s was driven by empirical results.

KNOWLEDGE THROUGH THEORY ALONE?

Economic knowledge is derived in different ways. The discussion so far has discussed testing against evidence, but the view is also taken that economic knowledge can be derived directly from economic theory in two ways. The first way is to base economic theories on what is known, seemingly with certainty, about human behaviour. The assumptions that people prefer some things to others and that they choose the most preferred option out of all the feasible options hardly need justification. We know such things by virtue of being human. Perhaps some people do not have preferences for different things, but they are generally seen as abnormal. If, therefore, we can construct theories that are based on assumptions like this, they should have explanatory power and they might even provide causal explanations, though for this we may need to know more about the environment in which choices are made.

The second way in which it is claimed that economists can derive knowledge directly from theory is through working with theories about ideal worlds that are not intended to represent the real world. General equilibrium theory is the clearest example of this. Some of the economists who developed it have said that if someone thinks it describes the real world, they do not understand it. The classic statement of general equilibrium theory, the so-called Arrow-Debreu model, describes a world that could not *possibly* exist: in an Arrow-Debreu world, there would be no reason for money to exist, and all transactions effectively have taken place simultaneously, at the beginning of time. Yet the same economists would argue that the model creates knowledge: it shows, for example, what would be necessary for the 'invisible hand' of the market mechanism to work perfectly, and hence why the presumption must be that markets do not allocate resources efficiently.

However, like empirical methods for testing economic theories, the methods of economic theory have their own problems. It may be true that human beings have preferences and make choices, but this does not imply that people are rational. Moreover, to get results, it is necessary to make further assumptions about the environment in which decisions are taken. The danger is that, though a theory may be presented as being based on the logic of choice – that is, on assumptions that are self-evidently true – other assumptions that should be questioned or tested against evidence will be brought in surreptitiously. The same is also true of the 'negative' results derived from models of ideal worlds. There is thus no short-cut around the need to test economic theories.

HOW ECONOMIC MODELS ARE USED

Because economic knowledge is derived in so many different ways, all of which have both something to offer and limitations, results derived from model-building, whether theoretical or empirical, always need to be supplemented by informed judgements for which there are no precise rules. There are limits to what can be said rigorously. The door is left wide open for critics to focus on the formal methods, paying insufficient attention to the informal, often poorly articulated, processes by which formal models are used. Thus many of the heterodox economists discussed in Chapter 9 reject outright the use of formal models. This tendency to pay insufficient attention to the informal processes by which different types of economic knowledge are evaluated is exacerbated because, for obvious reasons, a training in economics emphasizes the technical aspects of the discipline. Students are taught how to construct and manipulate formal models in both economic theory and econometrics, but the procedures by which those models are used are not so fully articulated. Students instead have to learn them not by being taught a set of rules but by observing and following the examples set by successful practitioners.

The argument that economic knowledge does not emerge mechanically and inexorably from using formal techniques but requires the informal balancing of evidence and exercise of judgement, is a theme that recurs in the examples of economics in action discussed in Chapters 2–5. In case after case, models informed decisions but did not dictate them. This naturally raises the question of what modelling contributes. Might it not be possible to dispense with models, relying on common-sense reasoning instead?

This issue has been addressed by the Bank of England (1999, p. 3) in a document explaining how they use economic models.

Why bother with models at all? Could policy judgments not simply be based on observation of current economic developments, in the light of lessons from past experience of how the economy works? That is indeed the basis for policy judgments, but making them without the aid of models would be extraordinarily difficult, not simple. ... Well-chosen models simplify and clarify economic problems by focusing on the factors judged most essential to their understanding. Crucially, models are also frameworks for empirical quantification – both of how the economy has on average behaved in the past, and of the degree to which its current or prospective behaviour might differ. For these general but practical reasons, monetary policy needs economic models.

A large econometric forecasting model is central to the Bank's inflation forecasts, but it is supplemented by other models, some based on economic theory, others that are purely statistical, based on patterns in the data. These simpler models serve as a check on results generated by the main model, they help forecast variables, such as trends in the world economy, that need to be fed into the main model, and they assist with problems on which the main model is silent. In this pluralist 'suite of models' approach, judgement plays a central role, that the Bank illustrates (1999, p. 7) with the following flow chart. Not only are policy decisions (changes in the interest rate or decisions to inject more money into the economy) informed by judgements as well as by forecasts, but the forecasts also embody judgements as well as outputs of the model, and other models inform the forecasters' and the policymakers' judgements.

Though it is rarely spelled out in the same detail, the same could be said, *mutatis mutandis*, about the use of models in other situations. The design of the 3G telecommunications spectrum auction (discussed in Chapter 2), was the outcome of auction theory and experimental results. In the case of the Russian transition (Chapter 3) and policies in relation to globalization (Chapter 4) the role of theory was more limited, because these problems involved a far broader range of issues.

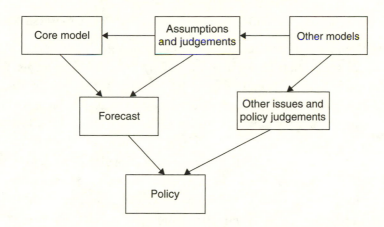

Of course, these methodological arguments do not prove that economists are successful even when they are aware of the dangers that may arise from the mechanical application of economic knowledge derived through their theoretical or empirical practices. That has to be decided by looking at what happens when economics is used in practice, as was done in Chapters 2–5. The conclusions reached there were that economics has proved itself very powerful where problems are sufficiently narrowly defined, where the objectives are very clear, and where it is possible to change the environment so that it conforms with the assumptions of economic theory. In some cases, believing the economic theory may in itself be enough to change behaviour so that the theory works. When economic ideas are applied to more complex situations, on the other hand, it is arguable that economics, by some criteria, failed, usually by neglecting to take account of dimensions of behaviour that do not fit into the rational-actor, competitive-market paradigm. Thus, whereas it was possible in the United States and Europe to create the institutions necessary for new financial markets to work, in Russia, the breakdown of control, combined with the complexity of the task, meant that the new institutions necessary for the transition to capitalism were not created sufficiently rapidly or effectively for the transition to run smoothly. Economic theory may well have distracted attention from the changes that were needed.

TOWARDS A DEMYTHOLOGIZING ECONOMIC DISCOURSE

The limitations of any results derived from model building and the need for such results to be supplemented by informed judgements, for which precise rules cannot be provided, also opens the door to ideology. It seems hard to believe that ideology did not play a role in either the enthusiasm for planning in the immediate post-Second World War decades, or more recently, in the enthusiasm for market solutions. However, it may be more fruitful to avoid accusations of ideology and to focus on myths about the economy. The term 'myth' is *not* used here to denote something false; instead it denotes a deeply held belief, or an intuitive idea, (which may or may not be true) about the world. If we adopt this perspective, it is hardly controversial to suggest that if the evidence is ambiguous, and judgements have to be made, economists, like anyone else, will be influenced by myths.

Today, the world has become deeply commercialized, experienced the collapse of communism, and saturated with media that propagate a free-market message. As a result, the dominant myths, both within contemporary society and within academic economics, are the competitive market and inefficient or corrupt governments. Economists are well aware that neither of these is universally true, but new ideas that support these myths have an easier ride than the ideas that challenge them. This has not always been the case: in the aftermath of the Great Depression, it was widely accepted that the market had failed and that state planning was essential to solve society's problems. However, the myth that private activity is more efficient than public activity was furthered by the turmoil of the 1970s that battered the post-Second World War social-democratic consensus and by the onslaught against collectivism by the generation of thinkers that came to dominate public discourse in the age of Ronald Reagan and Margaret Thatcher. It was reinforced by the collapse of communism.

There is some suggestion that the dramatic events of the 2007–8 financial crisis, may have begun to dent that confidence. When Alan Greenspan, on 23 October 2008, was asked by a Congressional committee, 'You found that your world, your ideology, was not right – it was not working?', he replied:

Absolutely, precisely. You know that's precisely the reason I was shocked, because I have been going for forty years or more with very considerable evidence that it was working exceptionally well. (Mason 2009, p. 118)

Note that Greenspan concedes both that his position was an ideology and that it was buttressed by considerable evidence – it was not that he held a view that was determined by his ideology against the evidence, the two reinforced each other.

Another believer in the power of the free market, Richard Posner, a leading figure in the economic analysis of the law, similarly wrote of the financial crisis that 'we may be too close to the event to grasp its enormity'.

Some conservatives believe that the depression is the result of unwise government policies. I believe it is a market failure. The government's myopia, passivity, and blunders played a critical role in *allowing* the recession to balloon into a depression … but without any government regulation we would still, in all likelihood, be in a depression. We are learning from it that we need a more active and intelligent government to keep our model of a capitalist economy from running off the rails. The movement to deregulate went too far by exaggerating the resilience – the self-healing powers – of laissez-faire capitalism. (Posner 2009, pp. vii, xii)

The implication here is that some views are so deeply held that it takes major events to change them. It remains (in 2010) to be seen whether the events of 2007–8 have been sufficiently traumatic to affect economic thinking in the same way that the Great Depression did in the 1930s.

A further reason for favouring the term myth is that deeply held views may develop as much because of their intellectual appeal as for their political implications. Indeed, the two may be hard to separate. If we accept that explanations in terms of individuals' preferences have explanatory power, that individuals are rational and that society is made up of individuals, it is then a short step to arguing that explaining an economic phenomenon *means* explaining it in terms of rational choice. This view can easily lead to an emphasis on economic theory at the expense of empirical evidence, and to the dismissal of any theory that rests on different foundations. Combine this with the difficulties involved in rigorously testing economic theories, and the power of rational-choice economics becomes hard to resist (compare with the discussion by Willem Buiter cited at the end of Chapter 7).

The assumption of rationality, if taken to its limits, can lead to the conclusion that this is the best of all possible worlds, for otherwise someone would have taken action to change it. This argument has potential ideological implications. Because it is so contentious, it is worth noting such a view was expressed by a self-confessed conservative, the highly influential Chicago economist George Stigler (see also p. 147), when he argued that, even though 'economics as a positive science is ethically – and therefore politically – neutral',

the professional study of economics makes one politically conservative. ... I shall mean by a conservative in economic matters a person who wishes most economic activity to be conducted by private enterprise, and who believes that abuses of private power will usually be checked, and incitements to efficiency and progress usually provided, by the forces of competition. (Stigler 1959, pp. 522, 524)

This statement could be translated as saying that acquiring the intellectual values of a professional economist (valuing rigorous theory based on precise assumptions about rational individuals who compete with each other), one will reach conclusions that are favourable to free markets. If the assumptions are correct, this will result in theories that stand up to rigorous empirical testing, a further intellectual value inculcated in the economist's training. Stigler might well have said that training as an economist makes one a conservative 'because it should'. It is perhaps, then, not surprising that some of those who cannot accept his political views have turned their backs on orthodox economic analysis.

However, the point that Stigler does not consider is the possibility that training as an economist may foster an *unjustified* faith in free markets. The elegance, simplicity and power of the rational-choice perfect-competition view of the world may seduce economists into being insufficiently critical of free-market capitalism. Economists have discovered many reasons markets may fail, but these remain inelegant special cases, necessitating a pragmatic approach to a policy that, because it is challenging the dominant myth, is always on the defensive. This is the case being made by the numerous critics who, before and after the 2007–8 financial crisis, were arguing that economists' theories, centred on a world of rational agents, were to blame for the failure to see the crash coming.

If this view is accepted, what follows from it? One position is represented in a recent opinion piece.

Once the dust has settled, there is a strong case for an inquiry into whether the teaching of economics has been captured by a small but dangerous sect. (Larry Elliott, *The Guardian*, 31 August 2009)

Leaving aside the obvious issues about academic freedom, this is the response of many heterodox economists, who see the discipline as having been taken over by what was, at least initially, a small group. Drawing on material covered in Chapter 8, one might make this more specific by identifying the small group with either the Mont Pèlerin Society or the University of Chicago. Such a view would justify arguing that the institutions of the profession need changing so as to encourage greater pluralism, enabling heterodox voices, such as those considered in Chapter 9, to be heard more loudly.

The problem with this reaction is that it fails to address the reason why rational-choice theorizing became so widely accepted. It was not foisted on the profession by a small, ideologically committed group. It was accepted because it offered powerful, rigorous and apparently scientific methods that appeared to be successful in tackling economic problems. The economists using these methods held political views that spanned the political spectrum and included many who sought to improve the ways in which governments intervened in the economy, not to attack the idea that there should be such intervention. There was a considerable record of success, both in responding to macroeconomic turmoil in the 1970s and in 'the reinvention of the bazaar' during the 1980s and 1990s.

There is, however, an even more fundamental reason for not going down this route – or at least, not going too far. The most powerful challenges to the myths of rational agents and competitive markets have come from economists who are at the heart of the economics profession, such as George Akerlof, Kenneth Arrow, Paul Krugman, Paul Samuelson, Robert Shiller and Joseph Stiglitz. Their work has challenged some of the assumptions on which conservative conclusions (as defined by Stigler) rest. Whilst the assumption of rationality has intuitive appeal, it is surely just as obvious that we do not have full information, that some people know more than others, that some agents can decide on the price at which they buy or sell goods and services, that people are influenced by fashions, that one person's action may have a direct effect on someone else, and that it is not always possible to charge for a good. What these economists have done is to show that such 'obvious' assumptions are more than theoretical wrinkles – they fundamentally alter the way markets work.

Such a perspective makes economics messier because it becomes necessary to examine, on a case by case basis, how markets work and how possible remedies might operate. The result is that empirical work moves to the fore, and due to the complexity of many of the problems, this empirical work has to be undertaken very carefully. It undermines the vision of economics put forward by Lionel Robbins in which economic propositions are logical consequences of the fact of scarcity and which implied a trivial role for the empirical work. It may also explain the problems encountered recently by the dominant macroeconomic theory which, though the mathematics may be complicated, is based on a highly abstract and conceptually rather simple model.

The appropriate response to inadequate economic theories is not to abandon the attempt to be rigorous. It is precisely *because* economists such as Akerlof or Stiglitz had developed abstract theories of how markets worked that they were able to see that the common sense views of how financial markets operated were wrong. Problems arose not because economists were not challenging the status quo, but because the economists who did challenge it were not being listened to. This is the response to heterodox economists who, though they may well have ideas that turn out to be important, have often failed to develop the analytical tools that can demonstrate the usefulness of those ideas. In the same way it was *because* Keynes, over seventy years ago, indulged in academic theorizing that he was able, in conjunction with the shock of the Great Depression, to undermine prevailing myths about the natural tendency of an economy towards full employment. Economic theory and serious empirical work – economic science – are needed to analyse and at times to challenge the myths that underlie our common sense notions of the world.

Note on the Literature

In the text, referencing has been kept to a minimum. The following Note supplements those references. Several chapters, even though they are completely new, draw on my earlier work, listed here, in which much more detailed references to the literature can be found.

CHAPTER 1: INTRODUCTION

Surveys of graduate students and the AEA report on the state of graduate education can be found in Colander and Klamer 1987, 1990; Colander 1998, 2005; Krueger 1991. On objections to economics see the references cited in the text. Comparisons with psychology draw on Backhouse and Fontaine 2010.

CHAPTER 2: CREATING NEW MARKETS

The discussion of the U.S. acid rain program is based on Ellerman et al. (2000) and Oates (1992), and the UK 3G telecom auction on accounts by the participants, including Binmore and Klemperer (2002) and Klemperer (1999, 2002a and 2002b), though the interpretations are not necessarily the ones they would place on the events. It also draws to varying degrees upon McAfee and McAfee (1996); McMillan (1994); Milgrom (2004); Nik Khah (2008); and Thaler (1994), which cover auctions in other countries and auction theory.

CHAPTER 3: CREATING A MARKET ECONOMY

Work on which this chapter draws includes Åslund 1991, 1992a, 1992b, 1995; Åslund and Layard 1993; Freeland 2000; Hanson 2002; Milanovic 1998; and Wedel 1998. Wedel is particularly useful for anyone wanting a view of the role played by Western economists.

CHAPTER 4: GLOBALIZATION AND WELFARE

For a sample of the vast literature by economists on the problem from a range of perspectives, see Bhagwati 2002, 2004; Chang 2002; Dehesa 2006; Easterley 2002; Milanovic 1998, 2002; Panic 2003; Stiglitz 2002. The discussion is particularly influenced by Wade and Wolf 2002, and Wade 2004. On inequality, see Atkinson 1995.

CHAPTER 5: MONEY AND FINANCE

There are now a number of excellent accounts of developments in financial markets, some antedating the 'credit crunch', others following it. Ones used in the preparation of this chapter include: Akerlof and Shiller 2009; Fox 2009; Harrison 1998; McKenzie 2006; Mehrling 2005; Posner 2009; Shiller 2003; Stiglitz 2002, 2003; Tett 2009. Backhouse 2009 raises some questions about the notion of performativity that underlies the work of McKenzie.

CHAPTER 6: CREATING A 'SCIENTIFIC' ECONOMICS

This chapter brings together an account of the development of economic theory, covered in Backhouse 1998, 2002, 2008 and 2010b with discussions of scientific method. The best discussions on the changed perspective on science are Weintraub 1998 and Rutherford 1999. The changing definition of economics and its implications are covered in Backhouse and Medema 2009a, 2009b, and 2009c. On the origins of public choice see Medema 2000. A valuable account of economists changing perceptions of the market is Medema 2009.

CHAPTER 7: THE QUEST FOR A RIGOROUS MACROECONOMICS

General accounts are provided in Backhouse 2002, 2008 and 2010b. On Keynes and Keynesian economics, see Backhouse and Bateman 2006; Backhouse and Laidler 2004; Backhouse 1997, 2010a.

CHAPTER 8: SCIENCE AND IDEOLOGY

This chapter is based on Backhouse 2005, 2009. On the funding of economics (and the social sciences) see Crowther-Heyck 2006 and Goodwin 1998. See also Khurana 2007 and Fourcade 2009.

CHAPTER 9: HETERODOXY AND DISSENT

This chapter draws on Backhouse 2000, and reflects subsequent readings of Coats 2001; Lee 2009; Mata 2009.

CHAPTER 10: ECONOMIC SCIENCE AND ECONOMIC MYTH

The main argument is covered in Hoover 2001 and Backhouse 2007 and draws on ideas from Backhouse and Durlauf 2009.

Bibliography

Akerlof, G. A. 1970. The market for lemons: quality uncertainty and the market mechanism. *Quarterly Journal of Economics* 84(3):488–500.

Akerlof, G. A. and R. Shiller. 2009. *Animal Spirits*. Princeton, NJ: Princeton University Press.

Amadae, S. 2003. *Rationalizing Capitalist Democracy*. Chicago, IL: University of Chicago Press.

Arrow, K. J. 1951. *Social Choice and Individual Values*. New York: Wiley.

Arrow, K. J. and Debreu, G. 1954. Existence of equilibrium for a competitive economy. *Econometrica* 22(4):481–92.

Åslund, A. 1991. Principles of privatization. In *Systemic Change and Stabilization in Eastern Europe*. L. Csaba (ed.). Aldershot: Dartmouth.

—— 1992a. *Post-Communist Economic Revolutions: How Big a Bang?* Washington, DC: Center for Strategic and International Studies.

—— 1992b. *The Post-Soviet Economy: Soviet and Western Perspectives*. New York: St Martin's Press.

—— 1995. *How Russia Became a Market Economy*. Washington, DC: Brookings Institution.

Åslund, A. and R. Layard 1993. *Changing the Economic System in Russia*. New York: St Martin's Press.

Atkinson, A. B. 1995. *Incomes and the Welfare State: Essays on Britain and Europe*. Cambridge: Cambridge University Press.

Backhouse, R. E. 1997. The rhetoric and methodology of modern macroeconomics. In B. Snowdon and H. Vane (eds.) *Reflections on the Development of Modern Macroeconomics*. Cheltenham: Edward Elgar.

—— 1998. The transformation of US economics, 1920–1960, viewed through a survey of journal articles. In *From Interwar Pluralism to Postwar Neoclassicism*, eds. M. S. Morgan and M. Rutherford, 85–107. Durham, NC: Duke University Press. (Annual Supplement to History of Political Economy 30).

—— 2000. Progress in heterodox economics. *Journal of the History of Economic Thought* 22(2):149–56.

—— 2002. *The Penguin History of Economics*. London: Penguin Books. Published in North America as *The Ordinary Business of Life: A History of Economics from the*

Ancient World to the Twenty-First Century. Princeton, NJ: Princeton University Press.

2005. The rise of free-market economics since 1945. In *Economists and the Role of Government*, eds. P. Boettke and S. G. Medema, 347–84. Durham, N.C.: Duke University Press. (Annual Supplement to *History of Political Economy* 37).

2007. Representation in economics: introduction. In *Measurement in Economics: A Handbook*, ed. M. Boumans, 135–52. London: Academic Press.

2008. Economics in the United States, 1945 to the present. In *New Palgrave Dictionary of Economics*. 2nd ed., eds. L. Blume and S. Durlauf, 522–33. London: Palgrave.

2009a. Review of MacKenzie (2006). *Economics and Philosophy* 25:99–106.

2009b. Economists and the rise of neo-liberalism. *Renewal* 17(4):17–25.

2010a. An abstruse and mathematical argument: the use of mathematical reasoning in the General Theory. In *The Return of Keynes: Keynes and Keynesian Policies in the New Millennium*, eds. B. W. Bateman, C. Marcuzzo and T. Hirai. Cambridge, MA: Harvard University Press.

2010b. Economics. In *The History of the Social Sciences since 1945*, eds., R. E. Backhouse and P. Fontaine. Cambridge: Cambridge University Press.

Backhouse, R. E. and Bateman, B. W. 2006. *The Cambridge Companion to Keynes*. Cambridge: Cambridge University Press.

Backhouse, R. E., and Laidler, D. E. W. 2004. What was lost with ISLM. History of Political Economy 36(Supplement):25-56. In *The IS-LM Model: Its Rise, Fall and Strange Persistence I*, eds. M. de Vroey and K. D. Hoover. Durham, NC: Duke University Press.

Backhouse, R. E. and S. N. Durlauf. 2009. Robbins on economic generalizations and reality in the light of modern econometrics. *Economica* 76:873–90.

Backhouse, R. E. and S. G. Medema. 2009a. On the definition of economics. *Journal of Economic Perspectives* 23 (1):221–33.

2009b. Defining economics: the long road to acceptance of the Robbins definition. *Economica*. Online at http://www3.interscience.wiley.com/journal/120120192/issue.

2009c. Robbins's essay and the axiomatization of economics. *Journal of the History of Economic Thought* 31(4):57–67.

Backhouse, R. E. and R. Middleton, eds. 2000. *Exemplary Economists*. 2 vols. Cheltenham: Edward Elgar.

Bank of England. 1999. *Economic Modelling at the Bank of England*. http://www.bankofengland.co.uk/publications/other/beqm/modcobook.htm.

Bernanke, B. S. 1981. Bankruptcy, liquidity and recession. *American Economic Review* 71(2):155–9.

2004. The great moderation. Online at http://www.federalreserve.gov/Boarddocs/Speeches/2004/20040220/default.htm.

Bernstein, M. 2001. *A Perilous Progress: Economics and the Public Purpose in Twentieth-Century America*. Princeton, NJ: Princeton University Press.

Bhagwati, J. 2002. *The Wind of the Hundred Days: How Washington Mismanaged Globalization*. Cambridge, MA: MIT Press.

2004. *In Praise of Globalization*. Oxford: Oxford University Press.

Binmore, K. and P. Klemperer (2002). The biggest auction ever: the sale of British 3G telecom licences. *Economic Journal* 112(478): C74-C96.

Burns, A. and W. C. Mitchell. 1945. *Measuring Business Cycles*. New York: NBER.

Chang, H.-J. 2002. *Kicking Away the Ladder: Development Strategy in Historical Perspective*. London: Anthem Press.

Coats, A. W. B. 2001. The AEA and the radical challenge to American social science. *Economics Broadly Considered: Essays in Honor of Warren J. Samuels*. eds. J. E. Biddle, J. B. Davis and S. G. Medema. London: Routledge: 144–58.

Cockett, R. (1994) *Thinking the Unthinkable: Think Tanks and the Economic Counter-Revolution, 1931–1983*. London: Harper Collins.

Colander, D. 1998. The sounds of silence: the profession's response to the COGEE report. *American Journal of Agricultural Economics* 80(3):600–7.

2005. The making of an economist redux. *Journal of Economic Perspectives* 19(1):175–98.

Colander, D. and A. Klamer. 1987. The making of an economist. *Journal of Economic Perspectives* 1(4):95–111.

1990. *The Making of an Economist*. Boulder, CO: Westview Press.

Coyle, D. 2004. *Sex, Drugs and Economics*. London: Texere Publishing.

2007. *The Soulful Science*. Princeton, NJ: Princeton University Press.

Crowther-Heyck, H. 2006. Patrons of the revolution: ideals and institutions in postwar behavioral science. *Isis* 97(3):420–46.

Dehesa, G. de la. 2006. *Winners and Losers in Globalization*. Oxford: Blackwell.

Easterley, W. 2002. *The Elusive Quest for Growth: Economists' Adventures and Misadventures in the Tropics*. Cambridge: MA: MIT Press.

Edwards, L. 1997. *The Power of Ideas: The Heritage Foundation at 25 Years*. Ottawa, IL: Jameson Books.

Eichner, A. and J. A. Kregel. 1975. An essay on post-Keynesian economics: a new paradigm in economics. *Journal of Economic Literature* 13(4):1294–314.

Ellerman, A. D., P. L. Joskow, et al. 2000. *Markets for Clean Air: The US Acid Rain Program*. Cambridge: Cambridge University Press.

Fox, J. 2009. *The Myth of the Rational Market*. New York: Harper Collins.

Frank, R. 2008. *The Economic Naturalist: Why Economics Explains Almost Everything*.

Fourcade, M. 2009. *Economists and Societies: Discipline and Profession in the United States, Britain and France, 1890s to 1990s*. Princeton, NJ: Princeton University Press.

Freeland, C. 2000. *Sale of the Century: The Inside Story of the Second Russian Revolution*. London: Little, Brown.

Friedman, M. 1953. The methodology of positive economics. In *Essays in Positive Economics*, ed. M. Friedman. Chicago: Chicago University Press.

1956. The quantity theory of money: a restatement. In *Studies in the Quantity Theory of Money*, ed. M. Friedman. Chicago: University of Chicago Press.

1968. The role of monetary policy. *American Economic Review* 58(1):1–17.

Friedman, M. and R. Friedman. 1979. *Free to Choose*: A Personal Statement. New York: Harcourt Brace.

Friedman, M., and A. J. Schwartz. 1963. *A Monetary History of the United States, 1861–1960*. Princeton, NJ: Princeton University Press.

Frost, G. 2002. *Anthony Fisher: Champion of Liberty*. London: Profile Books.

Fulbrook, E. (ed.) 2004. *A Guide to What's Wrong with Economics*. London: Anthem Press.

Galbraith, J. K. 1952. *American Capitalism: The Concept of Countervailing Power*. London: Penguin Books.

1957. *The Affluent Society*. London: Penguin Books.

1967. *The New Industrial State*. London: Penguin Books.

Goodwin, C. D. W. 1998. The patrons of economics in a time of transformation. In *From Interwar Pluralism to Postwar Neoclassicism*, eds. M. S. Morgan and M. Rutherford, 53–81. Durham, NC: Duke University Press. (Annual Supplement to History of Political Economy 30).

Hanson, P. 2002. Barriers to long-run growth in Russia. *Economy and Society* 31(1):62–84.

Harford, T. 2008. *The Logic of Life: The New Economics of Everything*. London: Abacus.

Harrison, P. 1998. A history of intellectual arbitrage: the evolution of financial economics. *History of Political Economy* 19 (Supplement: New Economics and Its History): 172–87.

Hayek, F. A. 1944. *The Road to Serfdom*. London: Routledge and Kegan Paul.

Hendry, D. F. and M. S. Morgan, eds. 1995. *The Foundations of Econometric Analysis*. Cambridge: Cambridge University Press.

Hoover, K. D. 2001. *The Methodology of Empirical Macroeconomics*. Cambridge: Cambridge University Press.

IMF, World Bank, et al. 1990. *The Economy of the USSR*. Washington, DC: World Bank.

Kay, J. 2004. *Everlasting Light Bulbs: How Economics Illuminates the World*. London: Erasmus Press.

Keuzenkamp, H. A., and J. Magnus. 1995. On Tests and Significance in Econometrics. *Journal of Econometrics* 67(1):103–28.

Keynes, J. M. 1936. *The General Theory of Employment, Interest and Money*. London: Macmillan.

Khurana, R. 2007. *From Higher Aims to Hired Hands: The Social Tranformation of American Business Schools and the Unfulfilled Promise of Management as a Profession*. Princeton, NJ: Princeton University Press.

Klamer, A. 1984. *The New Classical Macroeconomics*. Brighton, UK: Harvester Press.

Klein, N. 2000. *No Logo: Solutions for a Solid Planet*. London: Flamingo.

Klein, P. 2006. *Economics Confronts the Economy*. Cheltenham: Edward Elgar.

Klemperer, P. 1999. Auction theory: a guide to the literature. *Journal of Economic Surveys* 13(3):227–86.

2002a. How not to run auctions: the European 3G telecom auctions. *European Economic Review* 46(4–5):829–45.

2002b. What really matters in auction design. *Journal of Economic Perspectives* 16(1):169–89.

Koopmans, T. C. 1957. *Three Essays on the State of Economic Science*. New York: McGraw Hill.

Kregel, J. A. 1973. *The Reconstruction of Political Economy: An Introduction to Post-Keynesian Economics*. London: Macmillan.

Krueger, A. et al 1991. Report of the Commission on Graduate Education in Economics. *Journal of Economic Literature* 29(3):1035–53.

Krugman, P. 1999. *The Return of Depression Economics*. London: Allen Lane.

2008. *The Return of Depression Economics and the Crisis of 2008*. London: Penguin.

Kuhn, T. S. 1970. *The Structure of Scientific Revolutions*. Chicago: Chicago University Press.

Landsberg, S. 2007. *More Sex is Safer Sex: The Unconventional Wisdom of Economics*. New York: Free Press.

Lawson, T. 1997. *Economics and Reality*. London: Routledge.

Lee, F. 2009. *A History of Heterodox Economics: Challenging the Mainstream in the Twentieth Century*. London: Routledge.

Leijonhufvud, A. 1968. *On Keynesian Economics and the Economics of Keynes*. Oxford: Oxford University Press.

Levitt, S. and Dubner, S. 2006. *Freakonomics: A Rogue Economist Explains the Hidden Side of Everything*. London: Penguin Books.

Lichtenstein, S. and Slovic, P. 1971. Reversals of preference between bids and choices in gambling decisions. *Journal of Experimental Psychology* 89:46–55.

Lucas, R. E. 1972. Expectations and the neutrality of money. *Journal of Economic Theory* 4 (2):103–24.

1976. Econometric policy evaluation: a critique. In *The Phillips Curve and Labor Markets*, eds. K. Brunner and A. Meltzer. Amsterdam: North-Holland.

Malinvaud, E. 1977. *The Theory of Unemployment Reconsidered*. Oxford: Basil Blackwell.

Marglin, S. 2008. *The Dismal Science: How Thinking Like an Economist Undermines Community*. Cambridge, MA: Harvard University Press.

Marshall, A. 1920. *The Principles of Economics*. 8th ed. London: Macmillan.

Mason, P. 2009. *Meltdown: The End of the Age of Greed*. London: Verso.

Mata, T. 2009. Migrations and boundary work: Harvard, radical economists, and the Committee on Political Discrimination. *Science in Context* 22 (1):115–43.

McAfee, R. P. and J. McAfee (1996). Analyzing the airwaves auction. *Journal of Economic Perspectives* 10(1):159–75.

McKenzie, D. 2006. *An Engine Not a Camera: How Financial Models Shape Markets*. Cambridge, MA: MIT Press.

McMillan, J. 1994. Selling spectrum rights. *Journal of Economic Perspectives* 8(3): 145–62.

2002. *Reinventing the Bazaar: A Natural History of Markets*. New York: WW Norton.

Medema, S. G. 2000. 'Related disciplines': the professionalization of public choice analysis. In *Toward a History of Applied Economics*, eds. R. E. Backhouse and J. Biddle, 289–323. Durham, NC: Duke University Press. (Annual Supplement to History of Political Economy, Volume 32.)

    2009. *The Hesitant Hand: Taming Self Interest in the History of Economic Ideas.* Princeton, NJ: Princeton University Press.

Mehrling, P. G. 2005. *Fischer Black and the Revolutionary Theory of Finance.* Hoboken, NJ: Wiley.

Milanovic, B. 1998. *Income, Inequality, and Poverty during the Transition from Planned to Market Economy.* Washington, DC: World Bank.

    2002. True world income distribution, 1988 and 1993: first calculation based on household surveys alone. *Economic Journal* 112(January):51–92

Milgrom, P. R. 1989. Auctions and bidding. *Journal of Economic Perspectives* 3:3–22.

    2004. *Putting Auction Theory to Workd.* Cambridge: Cambridge University Press.

Neumann, J. von. and O. Morgenstern. 1944. *The Theory of Games and Economic Behavior.* Princeton, NJ: Princeton University Press.

Nik-Khah, E. 2008. A Tale of Two Auctions. *Journal of Institutional Economics* 4(1): 73–97.

Oates, W. E., ed. 1992. *The Economics of the Environment.* Aldershot, UK: Edward Elgar.

Ormerod, P. 1994. *The Death of Economics.* London: Faber and Faber.

Panić, M. 2003. *Globalization and National Economic Welfare.* London: Palgrave.

Patinkin, D. 1956. *Money, Interest and Prices.* Evanston, Il: Row, Peterson.

Phelps, E. S. et al. 1970. *Microeconomic Foundations of Employment and Inflation Theory.* London: Macmillan.

Phillips, A. 1962. Operations research and the theory of the firm. *Southern Economic Journal* 28(4):357–64.

Polak, J. J. 1997. The contribution of the International Monetary Fund. In *The Post-1945 Internationalization of Economics*, ed. A. W. B. Coats, 211–24. Durham, NC: Duke University Press.

Posner, R. A. 2009. *A Failure of Capitalism: The Crisis of '08 and the Descent into Depression.* Cambridge, MA: Harvard University Press.

Reder, M. W. 1982. Chicago economics: permanence and change. *Journal of Economic Literature* 20:1–38.

Robbins, L. C. 1932. *An Essay on the Nature and Significance of Economic Science.* London: Macmillan.

Rutherford, M. 1999. Institutionalism as 'scientific' economics. In *From Classical Economics to the Theory of the Firm: Essays in Honour of D. P. O'Brien*, eds. R. E. Backhouse and J. Creedy, 223–42. Cheltenham: Edward Elgar.

Samuelson, P. A. 1947. *Foundations of Economic Analysis.* Cambridge, MA: Harvard University Press.

Shiller, R. 2003. *Irrational Exuberence.* Princeton, NJ: Princeton University Press.

Stigler, G. J. 1959. The politics of political economists. *Quarterly Journal of Economics* 73 (4):522–32.

Stiglitz, J. E. 1994. *Whither Socialism?* Cambridge, MA, MIT Press.

    2002. *Globalization and its Discontents.* London: Allen Lane.

    2003. *The Roaring Nineties: Seeds of Destruction.* London: Allen Lane.

Tett, G. 2009. *Fool's Gold: How Unrestrained Greed Corrupted a Dream, Shattered Global Markets, and Unleashed a Catastrophe.* London: Little Brown.

Thaler, R. 1994. *The Winner's Curse: Paradoxes and Anomalies of Economic Life.* Princeton, NJ: Princeton University Press.

Wade, R. H. 2004. Is globalization reducing poverty and inequality? *World Development* 32 (4):567–89.

Wedel, J. 1998. *Collision and Collusion: The Strange Case of Western Aid to Eastern Europe, 1989 – 1998.* London: Macmillan.

Weintraub, E. R. 1998. Axiomatisches missverstaendniss. *Economic Journal* 108:1837–47.

Williamson, J., ed. 1994. *The Political Economy of Policy Reform.* Washington, DC: Institute for International Economics.

Wolf, M. 2004. *Why Globalization Works.* New Haven, CT: Yale University Press.

Wolf, M. and R. H. Wade. 2002. Are global poverty and inequality getting worse? *Prospect Magazine* 72:16–21.

World Bank. 2000. *World Development Report, 2000–2001: Attacking Poverty.* Oxford: Oxford University Press.

Index

acid rain program, 16, 22–27, 50
Adam Smith Institute, 142
Affluent Society (Galbraith 1957), 157
Akerlof, George, 110, 185, 186
Amadae, Sonja, 144
American Capitalism (Galbraith 1952), 157
American Economic Association (AEA), 6, 128, 158, 159, 160
    Commission on Graduate Education in Economics (COGEE), 7
American Economic Review, 11
American Enterprise Institute (AEI), 141, 142
American International Group (AIG), 92
Analysis and Research Association (ARA), 143
arbitrage, 75, 80, 82, 83, 84, 93, 194
Arrow, Kenneth J., 104–05, 106, 107, 110, 123, 124, 133, 145, 147, 185
Arrow-Debreu model, 105, 178
Åslund, Anders, 39, 40, 41
Association of Heterodox Economics, 161
Atkinson, Anthony, 65, 66
Atlas, 142
auction theory, 29, 30–31, 34, 180
auctions
    English and Dutch, 29, 30, 31, 32
    outside the UK, 33
Australia, 84
Austrian economics, 154, 160

Bach, Lee, 146
Backhouse, Roger E., 108
Bank of England, 85, 88, 90, 92, 93, 96, 135, 174, 180, *See also* monetary policy, in UK
Bank of Japan, 91
Barro, Robert J., 136

Bear Stearns, 91, 92
Becker, Gary, 111, 112, 148
Bernanke, Ben, 84, 89, 92, 134
Bernstein, Michael, 129
Besley, Tim, 94
Big Bang, 74
Binmore, Ken, 27
Black, Fischer, 76, 77, 78, 79, 82
Black-Scholes formula, 77, 78, 79, 80, 81
Blanchard, Oliver, 146
Blaug, Mark, 108
BNP Paribas, 91
Bourbaki, 105
Bradley Foundation, 143
Bretton Woods system, 53
Britain. *See* United Kingdom
British Academy, 94
Brookings Institution, 142, 143
Brookings Papers, 11
Buchanan, James, 111, 148, 150
Buiter, Willem, 135–36, 147, 184
Burns, Arthur, 125
Bush, President George H. W., 22
Bush, President George W., 95
business cycle, 117, 123, 125, 126, 132, 155, 156, 178

Card, David, 13
Carnegie Foundation, 143, 144
Carnegie-Mellon University, 129
Central Intelligence Agency (CIA), 102, 144
Centre for Policy Studies, 142
Chernomyrdin, Victor, 43
Chicago, 158
Chicago Board Options Exchange, 76
China, 36, 44, 60, 67, 69
Chubais, Anatoly, 39, 41, 44, 45, 46, 48
Church of England, 162

Patinkin, Don, 123
perfect competition, 48, 103, 107
performativity, 17
Phelps, Edmund S., 130, 178
Phillips, Almarin, 177
physics, 4
Poincaré, Henri, 100
Polak, Jacques, 146
policy intelligensia, 3
Political and Economic Planning, 141
political science, 4, 112, 154
Posner, Richard, 183
Post-Autistic Economics, 5, 6, 161, 163
Post-Keynesian Economics, 8, 13, 154, 159, 160, 161
poverty, 158
 and globalization. *See* globalization and poverty
 measurement of, 64
predictions
 Friedman on, 107
Prescott, Edward, 132, 136
Princeton University, 1, 10, 109, 134
Principles of Economics (Marshall 1920), 100
privatization, 18, 38, 39, 40, 41, 43, 44, 45, 54, 55, 58, 68, 141
protection, 60
psychology, 4, 18, 129, 154, 175
public choice, 62, 111, 148, 150, 161
Public Choice Society, 161
public goods, 106, 107, 111
purchasing power parity, 63

Quantity Theory of Money: A Restatement (Friedman 1956), 126

race, 158
Radical economics, 13
RAND Corporation, 109, 144–45, 146
Rapping, Leonard, 130
rational choice, 15, 16, 96, 112, 122, 144, 145, 147, 151, 169, 175, 183, 184, 185
rational expectations, 131, 132, 136, 147, 149, 150
rationality, 10, 16, 40, 75, 95, 96, 110, 112, 114, 122, 131, 132, 135, 145, 149, 169, 170, 179, 181, 183, 184, 185
Read, Leonard E., 141
Reader's Digest, 140
Reagan, President Ronald, 54, 143, 151, 182
real business cycle (RBC) theory, 132, 133, 154
Reder, Melvin, 149

Reinventing the Bazaar (McMillan 2002), 9
representative agent, 133
rigour, 99–100, 124, 133, 147, 149
 in macroeconomics, 117–36
Road to Serfdom (Hayek 1944), 140
Robbins definition. *See* Robbins, Lionel; economics, definition of
Robbins, Lionel, 100, 101, 112, 170, 186
Robinson, Joan, 157
Rockefeller Foundation, 143, 144
Rothbard, Murray, 160
Russell Sage Foundation, 141
Russia, 18, 37, 38, 39, 42, 43, 44, 46, 49, 69, 82, 102, 180, 181, 191, 194
Rutherford, Malcolm, 100

Sachs, Jeffrey, 39
Salomon Brothers, 74
Samuelson, Paul A., 104, 105–06, 107, 138, 139, 147, 157, 161, 185
Sargent, Thomas, 136
Scaife Foundations, 143
Scholes, Myron, 77, 78, 79, 81
Schwartz, Anna J., 126–27
Sex, Drugs and Economics (Coyle 2004), 2
Shiller, Robert, 95, 185
Shleifer, Andrei, 39
shock therapy, 39, 40, 42, 43, 44, 47
Simon, Herbert, 129
Slovic, Paul, 113
Smith, Vernon, 114
Social Affairs Unit, 142
Social Choice and Individual Values (Arrow 1951), 105, 145
socialism, 156
sociology, 4, 18, 111, 112, 154
Solow, Robert M., 6, 160
Soulful Science (Coyle 2007), 2
Soviet transition, 18, 37–50, 180
Soviet Union, 137
Spain, 84
spectrum auction, 16, 17, 27–35, 180
Spence, Michael, 110
stagflation, 128
Stanford University, 3
statistics, 168, 172, 173
Stigler, George J., 108, 109, 147, 156, 184, 185
Stiglitz, Joseph, 48, 61, 95, 110, 147, 162, 185, 186
stock market crash, October 1987 81, 87
Structure of Scientific Revolutions (Kuhn 1962/1970), 158
sub-prime mortgage crisis, 17, 91
sulphur dioxide. *See* acid rain program (US)